FAR BEYOND GOLD

FAR BEYOND GOLD

RUNNING FROM FEAR TO FAITH

SYDNEY MCLAUGHLIN-LEVRONE

W PUBLISHING GROUP

AN IMPRINT OF THOMAS NELSON

Published in Nashville, Tennessee, by W Publishing, an imprint of Thomas Nelson.

Author represented by Mel Berger, WME.

Thomas Nelson titles may be purchased in bulk for educational, business, fundraising, or sales promotional use. For information, please email SpecialMarkets@ ThomasNelson.com.

Unless otherwise noted, Scripture quotations are taken from the ESV® Bible (The Holy Bible, English Standard Version®). Copyright © 2001 by Crossway, a publishing ministry of Good News Publishers. Used by permission. All rights reserved.

Scripture quotations marked NIV are taken from the Holy Bible, New International Version®, NIV®. Copyright © 1973, 1978, 1984, 2011 by Biblica, Inc.® Used by permission of Zondervan. All rights reserved worldwide. www.zondervan.com. The "NIV" and "New International Version" are trademarks registered in the United States Patent and Trademark Office by Biblica, Inc.®

Scripture quotations marked NLT are taken from the Holy Bible, New Living Translation. Copyright © 1996, 2004, 2015 by Tyndale House Foundation. Used by permission of Tyndale House Ministries, Carol Stream, Illinois 60188. All rights reserved.

Italics added to direct Scripture quotations are the author's emphasis.

Any internet addresses, phone numbers, or company or product information printed in this book are offered as a resource and are not intended in any way to be or to imply an endorsement by Thomas Nelson, nor does Thomas Nelson vouch for the existence, content, or services of these sites, phone numbers, companies, or products beyond the life of this book.

ISBN 978-0-7852-9799-4 (HC)
ISBN 978-0-7852-9897-7 (audiobook)
ISBN 978-0-7852-9829-8 (ePub)
ISBN 978-0-7852-9826-7 (TP)

Library of Congress Control Number: 2023941247

Printed in the United States of America
24 25 26 27 28 LBC 5 4 3 2 1

To anyone who has ever experienced crippling fear.
May the truth set you free.

Introduction

If you have decided to read this book, I'm guessing you know at least one fact about me. I'm "the fast girl," the one who can circle a 400-meter track more quickly than most, even when there are ten barriers I have to jump over. As long as I can remember, that fact has been the biggest part of who I am. I've always thought of myself as the girl whose feet can take her from point A to point B before everyone else. Over the years, it's how I've been identified by friends, teachers, and coaches. "That's Sydney; she's fast. Real fast."

I used to see myself almost exclusively that way. Nothing about me mattered, or frankly made much sense, if I wasn't winning a race. I had to live up to my identity as a winner. That, I thought, was the reason I was on this earth.

This book is about a lot of things. It's about my career on the track. It's about my personal life off it. It's about my greatest achievements and my worst failures. It's a behind-the-scenes look at how I train and what it has taken to perform at the highest level on the biggest stage. But at the heart of this book is a simple question: *Who is Sydney?*

Finding the right answer hasn't always been easy for me. It's involved years of inner turmoil. Loads of fear. And a whole lot of questions and uncertainty. I'm guessing you can relate to those struggles. All of us want to know who we are, why we are here, and what's going to make us happy and fulfilled. We want to have a purpose, a strong sense of identity, and clarity about how we are supposed to spend our days. Perhaps most importantly, we crave someone to love and care for, as well as to be loved and cared for, while we are here.

Of course, the answers to "Who am I?" seem to change. When we're younger, we're kids—a son or daughter. When we get older, we might become a spouse, then perhaps a parent, then a grandparent. At school, we are the athlete, the popular kid, the class clown, the honors student, or the outcast. At work, we are the intern. Then the entry-level worker. Then the manager. Then the boss.

I think most of us—maybe all of us—struggle to reconcile those different identities. I know I did. For years, I was one way on the track and another off it. I was one person in front of the cameras and in the press room and a different one in private.

Through a long journey, I've learned that my different identities, especially my identity on the track, are part of a single reality about me. This reality is not how well I've performed during my career. My main identity is that I'm a daughter of God. I belong to him.

For a long time, I didn't think much about honoring and

serving him. I grew up going to church and always believed in God to some extent, but in my everyday life, I still wanted to control everything. And I looked to other people for my value and peace. What resulted was constant anxiety. Debilitating fear. And, at times, depression.

By God's grace, those emotions do not consume me today. Yes, I still battle them. But they no longer have the control over my life they once did. This book will explain why. I want to share my story with you, from fearful teenage years, through a series of life-changing events in 2020, and into my life of faith and hope since then. Along the way, I'll take you behind the scenes of my life on the track and away from the track—my family, my marriage, my struggles, fears, hopes, dreams, and faith.

Why am I sharing all this with you? I want my story to encourage anyone who struggles with fear and anxiety. If God can turn me from fear to faith, I know he can do the same for you. Along the way, I'm going to show you how I came to recognize my fears and how you can spot the same anxiety in your life, then respond by going to the one who can set you free. I pray my story will point you in his direction and show you that no matter who you are or what you do, God is calling you to trust him, to let go of the struggle to define yourself or live up to other people's expectations. He wants you, no matter who you are, to find your identity in him and his Son, Jesus Christ.

If you're not a Christian or don't believe in God, I'm glad you're here. If you stick with me through these pages, you'll hear a lot about why I love track, why I'm grateful for my career, and what you can do to train, prepare, or work out stronger and smarter no matter where you are or where you're from. And if you give me the privilege of telling you my story, all I ask is that you consider where you get your sense of identity. Are you free of fear? Are you strong enough on your own? How could a relationship with God bring you peace, love, hope, and joy?

The story you're about to read is about a particular time of my life, from 2016, when I was a terrified sixteen-year-old at the Olympic trials in Eugene, Oregon, through the World Championships in 2022. During that six-year period, I experienced the lowest of lows and the highest of highs. I met my husband, got married, and accomplished a lot of my childhood dreams. Most importantly, I became a Christian. Those six years depict my life's encounter with profound grace. Freedom. Hope for the future. I pray all these things become true for you, too, as you join me on this journey.

Chapter 1

I almost didn't run the most important race of my life.

July 8, 2016. It was day three of the US Track and Field Olympic Team trials in Eugene, Oregon. One hour before the 400-meter hurdle quarterfinals were scheduled to begin. The first and, I figured, only heat I'd run, I completely lost my nerve. *These are actual professionals out here,* I thought. *There's no way I can hang with them.*

Every other woman in the trials had been training for this moment for years, and it showed. They had world-class coaching, big-time sponsors, strict diets, and meticulous workout regimens. I had none of those things. What I did have was a whole lot of teenage angst . . . and my lucky *Minions* blanket. I was only sixteen years old, a nervous, timid high school junior from

Dunellen, New Jersey—a quiet suburb thirty miles southwest of Manhattan. It was a great place to grow up, but not exactly home to a lot of Olympic athletes. I didn't know of anyone from my hometown or school who had been where my shoes then stood. Yet there I was, matched up against some of the fastest women on the planet. If I somehow made it through the first two rounds, then finished among the top three in the finals, I'd qualify for the 2016 Olympics in Rio de Janeiro, Brazil, and become the youngest member of the US Olympic track-and-field team since 1972. No pressure.

My parents, siblings, and I were staying at an Airbnb an hour from Eugene, so the first time I laid eyes on the packed stadium was eighty minutes before my first race began. I had a swirling pit in my stomach the entire drive to Eugene. Just a few hours earlier, I had woken up in the middle of the night drenched in sweat, battling anxiety. That morning, I had to force myself to eat breakfast. Thanks to the nerves, I cleared maybe a third of my plate. The lack of sleep, appetite, and energy was normal for me before big races. What wasn't normal that time—and what turned my manageable nerves into uncontrollable trepidation—was the crowd. It was easily the largest I had ever competed in front of. More than ten thousand fans gathered at Hayward Field on the campus of the University of Oregon. I was used to a smattering of faces in the crowd—parents, friends, teammates, coaches, and maybe a few scouts—but this was a sea of people.

As intimidating as the crowd was, it wasn't the ultimate reason I wanted to be anywhere other than Hayward Field that Friday afternoon. The reason I almost bailed that day was the other competitors. All around me I saw women who were bigger, stronger, more experienced, and, I assumed, faster than I was. They clearly had a strategy as they warmed up. I did not. I would run a bit from one side of the warm-up area to the other and stretch without rhyme or reason. I remember looking around one too many times and making eye contact with some of them. It was terrifying. They had equipment—so much equipment. All I had was a little backpack with some extra shoes and clothes. I had never felt so unprepared, so undeserving, and so uncertain of what I was supposed to do. As the race approached, I started hyperventilating, which brought on tears and led to a full-on panic attack. I slipped away from my Union Catholic High School coaches Mike McCabe and Luiz Cartegena and called my dad. I didn't want anyone to hear this conversation.

"Can I please pull out of this race?" I begged my father, feeling half my age. "I don't want to run," I told him, tears streaming down my face. "I promise I'll try again in four years."

"You're already there, Syd," my dad said in a calm, soothing voice. "Just make it through this round, and we'll talk about it. Everyone is here to see you run. Get the experience. It's the first round of three; there's no pressure on you."

When I ended the call, I knew there was no getting out of the race. So I found the nearest bathroom and threw up. Then I trekked back to the warm-up area and mechanically went through the rest of my stretches, desiring one thing: for this race to be over.

With the race a few minutes away, I tried to tell myself, "God's got you." It was a phrase I often muttered to myself before competing. Did he really have me in this moment, though? I wasn't sure how to know for certain. At this point in my life, my relationship with God had consisted only of childhood Bible stories, the "Jesus Loves Me" song, and basic knowledge that

God is good. So in a time when I truly needed him to guide me, I wasn't sure if he was even there. All I could do was hope that the invisible God I had been raised to fear would be there for me in a time such as this.

My mom later told me that she and my dad didn't know if I would even come out of the warm-up area until I appeared a few minutes before the race began. I emerged with a serious expression on my face. That's when something familiar took over. It's something that has been with me my entire life, since my first race, a 100-meter dash when I was six years old. Each time I take my position at the starting line, my body grows taut with anticipation, and every distracted thought, scattered plan, and overwhelming fear fades away. All that remains is a will, a desire, a desperate need to win. I hate losing. Always have. Always will. That's the one part of sixteen-year-old Sydney the fear could not touch.

> All I could do was hope that the invisible God I had been raised to fear would be there for me in a time such as this.

The 400-meter hurdles isn't the shortest race in track and field, but it feels like the longest. It's widely considered one of the most grueling events in the sport, often referred to as "the man killer." Because of the hurdles, you have to master the technique required to clear the barrier every fourteen or fifteen steps without losing balance or velocity. And the length is just long enough to demand extraordinary endurance while being short enough to require superior speed. If you want to win, you can't hold back or conserve energy. No other event requires that combination of technique, endurance, and speed.

At the starting line, I noticed a familiar face among the professionals lined up beside me: Kori Carter. She'd won the 400-meter hurdle NCAA national championship a few years earlier. The following year, 2017, she'd win the 400-meter hurdle World Championship in London. I'd never raced against someone so accomplished. She was the most talented runner in our heat, so I figured if I could hang with her, I would be able to survive this race. As the gun went off, there was only one thought repeating in my mind: *Keep up with Kori.*

Before I knew it, we were pushing down the backstretch, 200 meters to go. Somehow, I not only managed to keep Kori in sight, but I nosed ahead of her down the final stretch. As the crowd roared and I cleared the last two hurdles, I was no longer feeling any of my prerace anxiety or insecurity about whether I belonged. The need to win had taken over entirely. I call it *the instinct.* Something kicks in automatically when it's me versus anything. I crossed the finish line just ahead of Kori and the other six competitors. I'd won the heat.

You'd think beating all the athletes I'd been intimidated by one minute earlier would cure my fear. You'd think I'd now be confident I was going to breeze through the next heat and then qualify for Rio in the final. That may have been the case for the pundits. It wasn't the case for me. As soon as the race was over, the irrational denial returned.

That night, I couldn't help but smile when I saw my dad. I'd survived the one race he told me to run before I could come back to the table to negotiate the remainder of our deal. I wasn't surprised when he started explaining how easy I made the race look and that it was a privilege to be there competing and winning at such a young age. And I couldn't argue. So we were on to round two.

ON THE EDGE

The next day, it was déjà vu in the warm-up area. But like the day before, my competitive instinct kicked in. As soon as the gun sounded, I tore through the track, finding purpose in my desperation to be the fastest. I not only qualified for the final, but I won the semifinal heat as well. Oh boy.

By the grace of God, there was a day off between the semifinal and final. It may have been the longest forty-eight hours of my life. Back at our rental house, I watched a lot of Netflix. I talked to my boyfriend on the phone. I did everything I could to keep myself from thinking about the next day, which I now see as strange because I was on the precipice of something I had dreamed about since I was a little girl. I remember watching the Beijing 2008 Summer Olympics when I was eight years old, sitting on a small stool in our living room, enamored by the spectacle of the women's 4-by-400-meter relay. As the first runners took their places, the camera panned over the packed stadium of spectators. When the gunshot went off and the runners exploded from their blocks, I leaned forward toward the TV, imagining myself running beside Allyson Felix and Sanya Richards-Ross, track icons who took and kept the lead for the United States that day. When Sanya Richards-Ross crossed the finish line first, capturing the gold medal for Team USA, I jumped up and cheered, pumping my fists in the air.

"I'm going to do that," I called out to my mom, who was in the next room. "I'm going to win a gold medal at the Olympics."

"Okay," she said, smiling, then continued what she was doing. She knew I was serious. From that day forward, dreaming of Olympic glory was one of my favorite pastimes. It's the ultimate goal for every track-and-field athlete. Now, eight years later, I was on the cusp of accomplishing my dream and doing it at only sixteen years of age. Yet at that life-changing moment, I wanted to think about anything but the next day's race.

Since that time, I've often asked myself why I was so afraid. You may know that kind of fear: the kind that freezes you, stops you in your tracks, and makes you forget everything you've worked for and everything you want. It feels like a curse, as if it's completely out of your control. Why was this happening to me? Why, suddenly, did I want nothing to do with my dreams of Olympic glory? It wasn't because I thought I had no chance of making the team. By any objective standard, I was one of the fastest in the field. I had every reason to believe not only that I belonged but also that if I performed to my capabilities, I would punch my ticket to Rio. I wasn't afraid of disappointing my parents. They never pressured me into running. They never made it seem like their happiness depended on my success. My mom and dad were both incredible runners. In the early eighties, my dad was a three-time all-American in track at Manhattan College in the Bronx. He had come up just short in his own bid to represent his country, making it to the semifinals of the 400 meters in the 1984 Olympic trials. Still, I never got the sense that he was living vicariously through my running career.

If I wasn't afraid of losing or terrified of disappointing my parents, why was I dreading the finals? Fueling my fear was an idea I couldn't shake: a sense of identity that came to define me. As a sixteen-year-old, I'd convinced myself that my worth and value were intertwined with my performance on the track. It wasn't enough just to be a runner; I had to be a winner. I viewed victories as value. Somewhere along the line, maybe as I became a teenager and started to wrestle with all the change, uncertainty, and drama that comes with that time of life, I convinced myself that I was put on this earth to win. And in order to receive love and respect from others, I had to finish first. If I didn't, what good was I?

No wonder the Olympics fueled my identity crisis. Losing seemed inevitable. If I didn't lose at the trials, I was almost guaranteed to lose, or so I assumed, at the actual Olympics. That hadn't been the case in the races I'd been running during the previous couple of years. Whether it was a track meet through my high school or the 2015 Youth World Championships in Cali, Colombia, I'd always been confident that if I did what I was supposed to, I would come out on top. That was because those races were familiar, and the competitors were my age. Since the competitive track scene is relatively small, I had raced against most of them before. It was all controllable and seemingly guaranteed to give me the outcome that would affirm my value. I'd pinned my entire sense of self-worth on being a winner. I had no idea at the time that there was another way to live. And that left me susceptible to fear.

There at the 2016 Olympic trials, everything was unknown and outside my control. I didn't previously know any of my competitors. I had no clue what it was like racing before such a massive crowd. I'd never run on national television, faced questions from reporters, or signed autographs. Instead of embracing the uncertainty and the very real possibility of failure, I

> I'd pinned my entire sense of self-worth on being a winner. I had no idea at the time that there was another way to live.

wanted to get away from it. But through the first two rounds, that had proven to be impossible.

Despite the fear, something clicked the night before the final race. It wasn't that suddenly my anxiety had gone away and I was now as light as a feather. That didn't happen. What did happen was a perspective shift. I realized there must have been a reason I made it this far. Though the lead-up to racing was dreadful, the gift always performed. All these grown women were probably more afraid of me than I was of them. Why? Because they had more to lose getting beat by a high school junior than I did losing to them. That change in my mindset took the pressure off me and put it back on them. With that in mind, I decided to go for it the next day.

LASER FOCUS

The morning of the finals dawned overcast and cool. The 400-meter hurdle final wasn't to start until after 5:00 p.m. that night. It was going to be a prime-time, made-for-TV event. The late start felt like another hurdle. The anticipation of having to endure the day made the idea of being finished feel light-years away. I tried my best to stay occupied that Sunday by watching TV. Though my mind was distracted, I would still nervously tap my fingers and wiggle my toes. My parents and I didn't say much as we made the hour drive from our Airbnb to Eugene, which is typical in my family. *Doing* is always more preferable than *talking*, especially on race days.

My silent, zoned-in demeanor carried over into the warm-up and prerace areas. Before a race, I try to minimize how much I interact with people around me. It's easy to lose focus when you're worried about someone else. I'm not trying to be unfriendly; it's just that I don't know how to smile and goof around, then lock into wanting to beat everyone else on the track. Once I walk into that venue, my mind is set on what I am there to do. I'll save the smiles and laughs for after. I also know some competitors aren't afraid to play mind games, to say something they think will distract the competition and give them an edge on the track. If you're going to beat me, it would be because you were the faster runner that day, not because I got distracted watching you dance in the call room.

The trials took race introductions to a whole new level for me. Blaring music. Walkouts. And camera close-ups. Those absurd close-ups when, one minute before the race, a cameraman scurries onto the track. Sometimes he highlights a few of the competitors. Other times, he starts in lane eight and works his way to lane one, bringing the camera within a foot or two of each runner, pausing for what seems like an uncomfortably long amount of time as the television commentators introduce each racer. They then announce each runner's accolades, some as long as a grocery list. The majority of women play it up for the crowd. They smile. Wave. Even blow a kiss to show some personality. That's just not me. Believe me, I've tried.

When the camera zoomed in on me in Eugene, I didn't acknowledge it. My eyes were laser-focused on a spot off in the distance as I rocked myself back and forth, dealing with an abundance of nervous energy. I was hyperfocused on what I was about to do, which was give every ounce of my strength to beat the other seven women. For me, the competition had already begun from the moment we stepped into the call room. As the camera lingered on me during the introductions, the commentator said, "Her poise, not just her talent, is why I think she'll make this team and be the youngest Olympian since 1972."[1] I was sure going to give it a try.

Finally, the time had come. After the longest forty-eight hours of my life between the semifinal and final, the announcer called us into the blocks. I locked myself into position, motionless, hearing nothing but my own heartbeat. The gun sounded and the race began. Twenty-three steps to the first hurdle. Fifteen to the second. Both jumps were with my right leg. My usual pace and rhythm. But then I noticed the others' pace. It was fast. Really fast. Dalilah Muhammad had roared out to a lead. No one was going to catch her that day. To her outside, in lanes seven and eight, T'Erea Brown and Ashley Spencer were in second and third, tearing down the track as if we'd already reached the home stretch. That familiar instinct kicked in, and I picked up the pace, determined to keep the leaders within reach. Between the second and third hurdle, I did something I'd never done before in training or in a race. I took just fourteen strides before it was time to jump, this time with my left foot ahead. In an effort to stay with the other women, I had taken one less step between hurdles than I normally did. It was completely foreign. The instinct just wouldn't let me slow down. By the seventh hurdle, lactic acid began to set in, a unique agony specific to the race's last stretch. When I reached the tenth and final hurdle, Dalilah seemed like she was miles ahead. Ashley Spencer in lane eight was in second, a half step ahead of me. If I could keep my place, I'd grab that third and final spot on the Olympic team. But to get there, I had to push through the exhaustion. Yet deeper than the pain, there was something I loved about that moment: the ultimate test of the will and, arguably, the sport's purest seconds of competition. It was me against myself. Me against gravity. Me against seven other finely tuned athletes. There were no referees, judges, or subjective standards. Just a simple question: *Can you get to the finish line first?*

As I leaned across the finish line, still in third place, I officially became an Olympian. Two feelings rushed to my mind, one on top of the other. The first was relief that the race was over, that I didn't have to push my body anymore, that I'd made it to the end of the hardest week of my life. The second was panic. *I just made the team. What have I done?*

OLYMPIC-LEVEL TERROR

During the race, the instinct kept those negative thoughts at bay. But as I crouched at the finish line, hands on knees, gasping for breath, they all came flooding back. Someone handed me a small American flag. A reporter for NBC News gathered the three Olympic qualifiers—Dalilah Muhammad, Ashley Spencer, and me—for an interview. Through labored breathing, Dalilah and Ashley smiled and expressed nothing but gratitude and excitement. "I'm just so grateful and so blessed and so happy to be going to Rio," Dalilah said.

"I just wanted to qualify. I had nothing to lose. I'm just so blessed. So very blessed," Ashley said, before crouching again, putting her hands on her knees, still struggling to breathe. The race lasts less than a minute, but those who run it feel the effects for hours.

"And Sydney," the reporter turned to me. "At sixteen. High

schooler. All the records. But now you're going to the Olympics. What do you think?"

"I can't breathe," were the first words out of my mouth.

The reporter laughed, still holding the microphone to me, expecting, I'm sure, for me to follow the lead of Dalilah and Ashley, maybe add a hashtag before *blessed* to flash my teenager credentials. Instead, I gave him this: "I'm just happy it's over with. Thank you, though."

Maybe because of the novelty of my age or my less-than-enthusiastic response to making the Olympic team, the reporter came back with a second question.

"Can you describe the pressure you were under, and has it been relieved?"

I told him the truth. "The only pressure is the pressure I put on myself. I'm just glad I'm done. I can't believe this."

"Believe it. You're going," the reporter said, wrapping up the interview.

At that point, I was determined *not* to go to Rio. And I was ready to say it out loud to someone, though preferably not on TV.

The first familiar face I saw after the race was my mom. She met me in a processing tent, where family and friends had gathered either to console or to congratulate the athletes. The medal ceremony was moments away, followed by a press conference with the three qualifiers. After that, I would complete drug testing, then head to team processing to pick up my uniforms and talk about logistics for the trip to Rio. Since I was a minor, a parent had to be with me for my test. When I saw my mom, I didn't break into tears of joy or start gushing about how I'd accomplished my dream. Instead, as we waited in the tent for the medal ceremony, surrounded by dozens of people or so, I loudly announced, "I'm not going. You can't make me go. I already talked to Dad about it."

My mom put a hand on my shoulder. "Shhh Syd, not right now," she said quietly. "We can talk about this later."

We never got to have that conversation. After the medal ceremony, the press conference began. Most of the questions went to Dalilah. She had just run one of the fastest races ever and was going to be one of the favorites at Rio (she would go on to win the gold six weeks later). She deserved all the attention. Most of the questions that came my way were about my feelings. "How does it feel to be an Olympian?" was the big one. I, of course, hid my true feelings, especially when someone asked me if I thought the three of us Americans could sweep the podium in Rio. I didn't want to think about that kind of pressure. The expectation that I should be on the podium terrified me. But I tried not to let anyone see my fear. Instead, I gave an answer I thought they'd want to hear and moved on.

I was still in a fog, zoned out and thinking less about the Olympics and more about a cheeseburger and cheesecake. My track brain turned off the moment I crossed that line. At that moment, I was hungry.

Everyone seemed to be happier for me than I was for myself. To the reporters, the fans, and the Olympic officials, there wasn't a question of whether I would go to Rio. Why would I not want to be part of something every athlete, including myself, dreams about?

Following the press conference, I headed to team processing. Happy, smiling Olympic officials handed me bags of Team USA gear and asked me what days I'd be traveling to Rio. That meant that before I could have a moment of privacy with my mom and dad, I'd gotten my uniform and plane tickets. The decision had been made. I was an Olympian.

By the time I finally got to have a conversation with my dad, he told me this Olympics was less of a quest for gold and more of an amazing opportunity for someone my age.

"God's given you a gift," my dad said. "You qualified for the trials. Now you've earned a spot on the Olympic team. This is the perfect way to get the experience, to know what it's like to be an Olympian. To get used to the crowds, the attention, the media."

Dad, of course, was right. There were no expectations for me, a sixteen-year-old, to win a medal in Rio. No one would be disappointed, even if I didn't make it through the first round. Still, I felt like I couldn't just relax and enjoy the moment. I couldn't shake the fear and embrace my dad's perspective on what I was about to experience. Why had God given me this gift right now? I wasn't ready. Winning had come naturally to me over the years. I couldn't remember the last time I'd run a race without expecting to win it. I was the girl who got to the finish line first. And because I saw myself that way, I was petrified of the Olympics, where I was almost guaranteed to come up short. The monthlong buildup until my departure for Rio truly felt like a lead-up to the electric chair.

I might have believed in my head that God had given me a gift, as Dad said, but the meaning of that hadn't traveled to my heart. My parents raised us kids going to church twice a week, and they made sure we had all the religious education we could get. Yet, at this point in my life, God hadn't become real to me. I knew *about* him, but I didn't *know* him, not really. The fear, at that point, felt much more real. And as focused on winning as I was, I hadn't yet

> As focused on winning as I was, I hadn't yet learned the value of perspective.

learned the value of perspective. I didn't know how to enjoy an experience for the sake of that experience.

In the coming days, I would come to embrace my new identity as an Olympian as best I could. It wouldn't come, though, without feelings of unpreparedness and impostor syndrome. I couldn't come to grips with the inevitable journey that lay ahead. Without any real guidance on how to navigate it, that fear and sense of inadequacy would shape how I prepared for the next biggest race of my life: the Olympics.

Chapter 2

Those 54.15 seconds in Eugene changed my life. Just a third of a second slower, I'd have finished fourth and failed to qualify. Now all anyone wanted to talk about was the Olympics. Every day, someone would congratulate me for making it to Rio. I wouldn't say it was a seamless adjustment to my new reality. At first, I didn't know how to respond when people showered me with praise. (I still sometimes don't know what to say when someone approaches me on the street or in a restaurant.)

Of course, part of me did like it. I was still a high schooler, and something in me warmed to all the attention. But another part of me would have been thrilled if all the attention went away. Then I wouldn't have had to deal with the expectations that came with people knowing who I was, doing a double take when I walked into a room, or asking for an autograph.

My new reality greeted me at the airport back in New Jersey. A crowd of friends and classmates gathered in the terminal, holding signs. There was lots of cheering and constant hugs. I did feel loved. People said it was "so cool" what I'd done. They gushed about the amazing experience I was about to have, how awesome it was that I was heading to Rio. It seemed the whole world was more excited than I was for the Olympics.

I felt terrified the first few days after the race in Eugene. If I tried to imagine what the Olympics were going to be like, I could only picture myself failing. For that reason, I tried to avoid them altogether, pretending none of it was going to happen.

The day after greeting the well-wishers at the airport, I was brought to the Union Catholic High School gymnasium, my home turf, for a press conference. One of the first questions was, "How are you feeling? Has the reality that you're going to the Olympics sunk in yet?"

I don't remember exactly what I said. I'm sure I described some of my emotions accurately. Yes, I was excited. Also overwhelmed. And a little in shock. I hadn't really had a chance to process what just happened. All that was true. I was trying my best not to think about what I'd just done. Crazy, I know. Anyone would assume I was thinking about the fact that I was an Olympian. But every time Rio came to mind, I'd be right back in the warm-up area in Eugene, nervous and scared. Of course, I couldn't say any of that to the reporters gathered in the sweltering gymnasium that July. All I could give them were the politically correct answers. I said things like, "I can't believe this is real. Grateful for my coaches and family. Excited to go with them to Rio." (At least that part was true—I was genuinely thrilled that my high school coaches were going to have an Olympic experience.) The truth was, I was happier for them than I was for myself.

A few weeks later, I flew to Los Angeles to attend the ESPYs and a ceremony for the Gatorade National Girls Track and Field Player of the Year. I had found out I won that award back in June, when I had been in Clovis, California. I was wrapping up a workout when I nearly ran into my hero. Literally. Since watching her win gold in the 2008 Olympics, I'd admired Allyson Felix. She is one of the most decorated track-and-field athletes of all time, and she's also one of the most gracious, dignified people in the sport.

I believed I was meeting with a news outlet that day who wanted to ask me a few questions, then watch one of my practices. After the interview portion, I began my warm-up. My coach and I did some hurdle drills and sprints. They snapped photos and took video. As I was cooling down, that's when it happened. As I rounded the bleachers that were blocking my view of the rest of the track, I heard the faintest, "Hey, Sydney." As I turned to see who was calling for me, my jaw couldn't help but drop. I was in complete disbelief. I had watched and admired Allyson for years. Now there she was, holding the Gatorade National Girls Track and Field Player of the Year trophy, ready to present me with it. I don't remember what I said, if anything. It was the first time I'd ever met Allyson. I think I cried a little. Smiled a lot. It was a surreal moment.

There'd been some media attention after that award, but even then, the press was more interested in my upcoming shot at the Olympics than the award I'd just won. They wanted to talk about my chances in Rio more than my accomplishments the previous year. I tried to shrug off all the Olympic talk, acting as if the trials were no big deal. I told *USA Today,* "I have so much more running to do. I'm so young. The pressure is definitely not on me. I didn't even expect to be here at this point yet."[2] Pretending I wasn't feeling any of the weight was a way to cope. And I was good at it. I could convince others that I was fearless. I had a great poker face. Over the years, I'd learned how to project that version of myself even when I was feeling the weight of the world. In that *USA Today* article, and my responses to all the questions people asked about the Olympics, I was giving people what they expected to hear, not what I was actually feeling. That separation between my inward emotions and my outward demeanor couldn't have been more stark. Trying not to look weak, I put on a brave face and strived to sound and be mature, when inside, I just wanted to be a kid.

> I put on a brave face and strived to sound and be mature, when inside, I just wanted to be a kid.

The real me used fear as a defense against things I believed would bring harm. Anything that showed signs of being a red flag quickly became my cue to flee. I had this uncanny ability to turn a normal event into a fire drill. I was a natural-born worrier. In my eyes, everyone was bad until proven good. This cycle of thinking occupied most of my adolescence. It wouldn't be until my early twenties that I'd learn that the panic I had been indulging in for so long was a trap. As Proverbs 29:25 says, "The fear of man lays a snare, but whoever trusts in the LORD is safe." It would take me a while to truly believe it.

A HISTORY OF FEAR

Fear had always supercharged my conscience. If I did something that I knew my parents wouldn't approve of, I couldn't keep it from them. Even minor mistakes. If I was watching TV at my house or a friend's and something came on the screen that I knew my parents wouldn't approve, I would feel guilty and ashamed, and I couldn't let go of the anxiety until I'd admitted what had happened to my parents. I feared correction. Being told no or that I was wrong cut me to the core. I wanted people to always be pleased with me. When something came about that could derail that, it ate at me. Looking back, I think a lot of that came from my misunderstanding of God's character. With an overemphasis on the judgment part of the gospel, I often didn't value God's other characteristics, such as love, grace, and forgiveness.

I'll never forget when an afternoon playing with friends tortured my conscience. I was in elementary school at the time. A few friends and I were riding our bikes through the neighborhood when we stumbled on toys, still in their packages, in a white garbage bag outside a house. It was on the curb, just sitting there. My friends whooped with joy and started to tear into the packages, in awe of their good fortune. I expressed reservations.

"These toys don't belong to us," I said. "Maybe someone accidentally left these here and was planning to come back later for them."

My friends shrugged off my concerns. "No one would do that," they said. "Someone was getting rid of these, so they're free for us."

What they said made sense. After they scavenged through what they wanted, I saw a new doll in a box, completely unopened.

I wanted to take it so badly, but my gut was telling me that we should knock on the door and ask first. Still, since the garbage bag had already been ripped to shreds and my friends began riding off, I took it. As soon as I walked through my house's front door, I immediately regretted taking the doll. I couldn't shake the feeling that I'd stolen it. Riddled with guilt, I hardly slept that night. The next day, I went back to where we'd found the toys and knocked on the closest houses, looking to see if the doll belonged to someone who wanted it back. (I never found the doll's original owner.)

I had dozens of stories like that, moments filled with anxiety when I worried I was disobeying my parents, displeasing God, or making a fool of myself. In the weeks following the Olympic trials, those memories and the apprehension they represented were with me. And they were a huge but unseen part of my story that summer.

As more and more people observed the calm, stoic, confident demeanor I projected to the world, they asked me to talk about how I developed my competitive personality and my will to win. Suddenly, my childhood was of interest to a lot of people. There was an assumption that I was built differently. The media loves to feed narratives like this. It's good for business. They are looking for the ingredients of an athlete's success—the experience, lessons, obstacles, and influences that molded them into an Olympic athlete. They want to craft a narrative, tell a story about an underdog overcoming adversity or a talented prodigy not buckling under the weight of expectations. So what was my story? What did I tell reporters, or just curious acquaintances, when I was asked about my childhood, my path to becoming a sixteen-year-old Olympian?

Though I didn't have a deep relationship with God at the time, I knew to credit him for my success. I didn't earn it; I just had it. It was as much a part of me as my height and brown eyes. The gift of speed was evident back at my first-ever race, a 100-meter dash when I was six years old. All the ingredients of my future career were already there. There was the thick, wild, and curly hair pulled back into a ponytail, the way-too-serious expression on my face, and the competitive instinct.

What they didn't know was that even at that age, I was terrified of losing, of having failure attached to me. That was where it all began. Overwhelmed by anxiety, I begged my dad not to make me go through with that first-ever race when I was six and risk coming in second, missing out on the first-place ribbon.

"Sydney," he said back then, taking a knee near the starting line. "You can do this. You were made to do this." With his encouragement and promise of a Hershey's chocolate bar (with almonds, of course) if I finished, I went

> Even at that age, I was terrified of losing, of having failure attached to me.

through with the race and won. When my dad went to collect me at the finish line, one of the coaches who organized the event approached him.

"This your daughter?" he asked my dad, pointing to me.

My dad put his hands around my tiny shoulders and nodded.

"She needs to run with my team so we can coach her," the coach said. "I can make her run fast."

My dad just smiled. "She's already fast," he said as we left the track.

Even before that race, my mom and dad had already seen that God had given me natural ability. Mom first noticed it when I was a toddler. At the time, we lived two streets away from the elementary school where my older brother and sister went. We'd walk there to pick them up each afternoon. Before returning home, Mom would let us play on the school's playground (New Jersey–weather permitting). I had a thing for the monkey bars. At three years old, I'd fling myself from one side to the other, suspending my tiny body in midair. From there, Mom can remember me following my siblings wherever they went, running as fast as I could to keep up.

When I was even younger, a little over a year old, my dad would put me in the palm of his hand and walk around the house. I'd balance myself on his palm for long periods of time. I didn't train for the monkey bars and mentally prepare for the ride around the house on my dad's palms. I had a God-given ability to balance, and that ability showed up when it was time to run.

Whether it was competing at six years old or chasing my siblings, running at high speeds felt as natural as breathing. I didn't have to think about it; I just did it. And I was raised in an environment where that natural ability was allowed to flourish. I grew up in a "track family." Both my parents ran track in high school, and my dad competed in college. That's where he met my mom, who was the team manager because the school didn't have a women's track team. All three of my siblings ran track. Clearly, it's impossible to be a McLaughlin and not run competitively.

Before I had my own meets, I was going to my older brother's and sister's races. Watching Morgan and Taylor compete and wanting nothing more than to keep up with them gave me an edge when I was old enough to start running on my own. They were so dedicated to doing their best, it inspired me. Then having my spunky little brother, Ryan, chasing after me kept me on my toes as well. I still remember standing on the starting line at many of my earliest races, knowing exactly what I had to do. *Get on the line. Take your stance. And when the gun goes off, run for your life.* That's how I conceptualized it back then. I was so competitive, I'd convince myself, even when I was as young as six, that life itself depended on winning.

In the weeks between the trials and Rio, when someone would ask me how I became an Olympic athlete, I'd shrug, not really knowing what to say. I honestly didn't think I deserved any of the credit for my speed. Thanks to Mom and Dad, I had good genes and grew up in a stable home with a passion for track. And thanks to my two brothers and sister, I was surrounded by competitors. I didn't choose any of that. I didn't earn it. God gave it to me. Of course, having a vague sense of where my quickness came from didn't help me get rid of the fear. I didn't really know what that mysterious God who gave me speed was really like—his love and care for me. Without that relationship, fear was in charge.

ROOM TO GROW

I think many people assume that an Olympic athlete has always had a singular devotion to the sport he or she is competing in. For me, that wasn't the case. My childhood was filled with all kinds of sports and activities. This allowed me to try a lot of things to see what my niche was. I also believe a childhood that wasn't consumed by track allowed my love and passion to grow at a healthy pace. Not obsessing over results and progression allowed my body to develop at a natural rate. Injury and mental burnout weren't a concern. In fact, I often wonder if I would have made it as far as I have if I didn't take a two-and-a-half-year break from competitive running.

The break started when I was nine years old. A loss at the AAU Junior Olympic Games in Michigan in the summer of 2008 crushed me. It was the 200-meter. I'd run as hard as I could, but the other girls were just faster. I felt so embarrassed. Not being on a team, I was coached by my dad. If I had been on a club team, I may have run faster at that meet, but my father knew what he was doing in minimally training me. He was letting my gift blossom naturally through time and maturity. So while the other girls my age were training rigorously to prepare for this meet, my dad saw the long game for my career and allowed me to lose then to protect it.

When we returned to New Jersey after the meet, I told Dad I wanted a change. "I don't want to do the track circuits anymore," I said. He looked at me, surprised. He clearly needed some convincing. "I'll do other sports. I just don't want to do this right now."

I'll always be grateful for what my dad said next. "All right," he agreed. "You can run as little or as much as you want. But why don't you give track another shot in middle school?"

I nodded. It was settled. For the next two and a half years of elementary school, I took a break from track, participating in only a handful of local meets. By that time, my older siblings were on school track teams while I focused on soccer, basketball, and dance. I had taken ballet, tap, and jazz from a young age and would continue to through middle school. My parents believe my dance training helped my running by strengthening my legs and core, instilling a sense of rhythm (a big part of running hurdles), and giving me the ability to leap with balance and strength.

Though I didn't run competitively during that time, I improved dramatically as my body grew and I developed my stability, power, and coordination. When I reached middle school and returned to track-and-field meets, I wasn't burned out. I wanted to be there. Not having that kind of high-level competition for several years had made me miss it. I think athletes need a period when they miss their sport. Distance makes the heart grow fonder. They should find themselves daydreaming about it, wishing they could be on the track, field, court, or course. Their bodies should twitch in anticipation. Competition can be grueling. The mind and body need rest, sometimes a long one. That's especially true for young people whose bodies and minds are still developing. That's why I'm so grateful for that extended break, when I could just be a kid exploring other interests, not taking myself too seriously.

My relationship with my parents was something else I was asked about as I prepared for Rio. Did my mom push me? Was my dad a hard coach? The questions made me laugh. Track was never a fight in my house. It was as much a part of my family as dinner and church. Yes, my dad was my first and only coach until middle school, but he was far from the intense, obsessive, critical type. He was the opposite. Soft-spoken. Encouraging. He never pushed me. If I had to use one word to describe his coaching philosophy, it would be *simple*. He never complicated the sport. His only strategy was for me to run faster than everyone else. Of course, we would discuss running mechanics, but they seemed to be second nature for me. While other coaches might give a stirring prerace speech or go over strategy one more time,

Dad would just look at me, smile, and say, "Syd, be the butterfly." Dad's inspiration was Muhammad Ali's famous phrase, "Float like a butterfly, sting like a bee." To me, "be the butterfly" in Ali's phrase meant quickness, lightness, freedom, and joy. It meant stepping on the track and making sure no one could catch me.

When I think of my childhood, it's mostly memories of afternoons at the track with my dad and siblings. Dad would set up cones and run us through simple sprint drills. He'd show me how to swing my arms efficiently when I ran or improve my knee drive for greater speed. I enjoyed those low-key workouts with Dad and my brothers. We'd go over the basics, test ourselves on the track, and then go home. I never dreaded practice or found it taxing. Dad later told me that he wanted us to learn to run and love to run without being forced to run.

In the place of technique, strategy, and motivation, Dad had a stash of sayings. He would say, "Time is money, and money is time. It's time to make some money." Of course, it wasn't actually time to make any money when I was racing as a little girl, but I got his point. It was something he'd say right before a race to get a quick smile out of me. It was always just as good as the first time I'd heard it. When I would play soccer, I remember the same encouragement, over and over. "Syd," he'd shout from the sidelines. "Just get it and go." In other words, don't complicate things. Your job is simple. Get the ball, run past everyone, and put it in the goal.

With my dad's reserved, laid-back personality, he was never inclined to push me. But he also seemed to understand that I didn't need to be pushed. I was naturally competitive, born with a drive to succeed.

My mom, on the other hand, was the chief of the operation.

Everything logistical, from signing me up for competitions to packing snacks to figuring out race-day outfits, was all her. She made sure I had everything I needed to be successful in whatever sport I was doing; her attention to detail made the process easy for me because all I had to do was perform. She was always encouraging

I was naturally competitive, born with a drive to succeed.

after races, games, and recitals, and it complemented my dad's natural coaching style well. They loved being active parents, and that was good because they had some very active children.

The same was true of my siblings. Everything around the house was a competition. Sometimes board games would become shouting matches. The smell of pancakes on a Saturday morning would send us rocketing out of bed, desperate to be the first downstairs. If we could figure out how to turn a mundane activity into a competition, we would.

My relationships with my siblings were much different from my relationship with my parents. Where my siblings pushed me and teased me, made me tougher, Mom and Dad encouraged me and rarely demanded more effort from me. Instead, both of them, especially my dad, wanted me not to take myself too seriously.

On our way to one race when I was seven or eight years old, I told him I was terrified of losing.

"If that happens," he responded, "we'll get some food and go home."

Simple words. Profound perspective. Win or lose, life goes on. You've still got to go about life. You still need to take care of yourself and others. It's just a game.

My parents believed that God had a plan for my life. No matter how busy our lives were, church was always a priority. If I had a soccer match on a Sunday afternoon, I'd wear my uniform to church that morning, then head straight to the game. If there was a midweek service, we went. My parents' firm commitment to raising my siblings and me with Christian values played a huge part in our lives growing up. It helped keep me grounded as a kid, even if I didn't yet have true faith in God.

Those five weeks between the trials and the Olympics were the closest I'd come to burnout since I asked my dad if I could step back from running. For the first time since middle school, I desperately wanted a break. I didn't want to see a track or compete, especially not in the Olympics. Far from the simplicity of childhood and my dad's image of a joyful butterfly, things were getting ever more bogged down and complicated. How could I make sense of it all?

TIME TO BE A KID

Despite my dad's easygoing attitude before the Olympic trials, I put enough pressure on myself for the both of us. As a result, it had been a long, grueling season. High school indoor track starts in mid-December. Now it was nearly August, and instead of winding down, I was ramping up for the biggest, most intimidating race of my life. Alongside all the races, training, and travel, there were the sleepless nights I couldn't avoid the night before a meet, the disinterested eating before a race, and the pit in my stomach as I prepared to compete. I was burned out. All I wanted was to be a sixteen-year-old girl for the last few weeks of summer. I wanted to go to the movies. Eat whatever food sounded good. Sleep in. Just generally do lazy, teenage stuff. The discipline that is required to have a chance at doing something great sounded like too much work. So I didn't do any of that. Instead, I ate Twizzlers.

Not long after the trials, someone gave me a huge carton of Twizzlers. I don't remember how many strings were in the box, but there must have been hundreds. I set it up next to my bed so that whenever I needed a pick-me-up, it was right there. It was empty long before I boarded the plane for Rio. While I'm sure other athletes were probably tracking their diets, I was tracking my way to Wendy's, ordering cheeseburgers. I figured my skinny body could use the calories. Besides, I was still a kid. How bad could it really hurt? There was also plenty of ignorance in each bite. I didn't really care to know what foods would cause inflammation in my body. I had no clue that the foods grown-ups tell you to eat actually do help fuel you. I thought it was just something parents say so you can't enjoy life.

I did go to the track nearly every day, but my heart wasn't in it. I think my parents and coaches saw my lack of discipline, but they didn't push me or try to micromanage my food and training. I'm grateful they let me be a kid (as much as that is possible when you're headed to the Olympics). I probably would have pushed back with all kinds of teenage emotions if they'd demanded too much from me. They seemed genuinely happy that I was on the team and had no expectations for me once I made it to Rio. I believe they understood the weight of this moment. Too much importance placed on your performance at the wrong time can derail you from wanting to pursue it again at some point in the future.

There were times that July and August when I was more focused on my birthday party than the upcoming competition. I would turn seventeen the day of the opening ceremonies. The plan was to still be home on that day, so I decided to throw a party. This wasn't some small family get-together. I wanted everyone I loved at a glow-in-the-dark mini golf place. There were piles of pizza and hot wings. It was perfect. One last hurrah before I entered the cauldron. After a few hours of mini golf and pizza, we went back to the house and watched the opening ceremonies. As the American team entered the stadium, I waved a flag, glad to be pretending I was part of the procession from the comfort of home.

In the weeks leading up to our flight to Brazil, I lived out, in the worst way, a quote often attributed to Benjamin Franklin that I've thought about many times over the years: "Failing to prepare is preparing to fail." With each piece of candy I ate, with each half-hearted effort I gave at the track, I was setting myself up for an uninspired performance in Rio.

I didn't tell anyone how I was feeling that summer. How could I? The whole world was excited. My parents were so proud, especially my dad.

"Everyone's blowing up my phone," I remember him saying at one point, a big, proud smile on his face. "I feel like the mayor."

With my mom and dad, coaches, friends, and everyone I met telling me how happy they were that I was embarking on this journey, I dared not disappoint them. My family had sacrificed time, money, and energy. My parents had put my athletic career over their interests. They'd made this incredible opportunity possible. How could I tell them I was dreading it? The same was true of my coaches at Union Catholic High. They'd invested their personal time into this, and now they had the incredible opportunity to go to the Olympics. I couldn't let them down.

As Rio approached, fear stole one of the great seasons of my life. The Olympics are meant to be a celebration of the human spirit. I don't think there's another event, with the possible exception of the World Cup, that has as much power to bring the world together. And it's all for the joy of competition. *Privilege* only begins to describe what it's like to make the team and represent your country. Millions dream of it. I was about to experience it. Yet all I could think about was the very real possibility of losing.

> As Rio approached, fear stole one of the great seasons of my life.

Maybe you've had something similar happen. You've let fear steal a moment of joy because you were afraid of losing something or someone you loved. It may not have been an experience like the Olympics but maybe something just as meaningful for you: a new relationship, a promotion, or even an afternoon with family. Those blessings will become burdens if you let fear control you and convince you that something terrible is about to happen, that the relationship will fail, or you won't succeed at work. Fear does that because it's there to destroy, ruin, take away peace, and disrupt our relationship with God. Thankfully, you don't have to let fear control you. Neither did I. If I knew then what I know now, I wouldn't have put up with fear or let it take from me the joy of competing in the Olympics.

If I could go back and be sixteen-year-old Sydney again, I'd want to release the burdens I was feeling. I'd stop focusing on what I didn't know and couldn't control and embrace the run-up to my first Olympics with the joy of a child. God had given me this incredible opportunity. I would "be the butterfly," as my dad was constantly telling me. I would run for the pleasure of running. Compete for the joy of competition. Worship God and honor him with the opportunity I'd been given. Instead of zeroing in on how hard it was going to be running against the best in the world, I'd look around and see the blessings God had poured out on my life.

I didn't know how to do any of that as I counted down the days until the Olympics began. And I was unsure how to honor God and embrace his gifts because I didn't have the right perspective on God, Jesus, and the Bible. Sixteen-year-old Sydney didn't see clearly because she didn't see the full picture. I knew only bits and pieces of the gospel, the good news that God had, through Christ, redeemed sinners. Yes, I called myself a Christian. I thought I knew what it meant to honor him, but I wasn't truly a believer. I hadn't yet come to the end of my efforts to control my life and submitted to him. Still trying to be the master of my own life, it was no wonder I struggled with fear. Everything was up to me—or so I thought at the time.

Freedom from fear was possible; it was waiting for me. Hope was coming. God was going to teach me how to rely on him for everything. But those lessons and the joys that would come with them were years into the future. In 2016, I was just a child, unable to see the privilege God had given me. That would lead to a fateful decision on the track in Rio: a decision in the thick of competition that I never imagined I would make; a decision fueled by trepidation I couldn't shake.

Chapter 3

From the moment we left for Rio a few days after my seventeenth birthday, everything about the experience was brand-new. Though I'd traveled around the country some to compete in meets, I'd been out of the United States only once before, flying to Colombia a year earlier for the Youth World Championships. The eight-and-a-half-hour flight to Rio was the longest of my life. Before that, the most time I'd been on a plane was five and a half hours just a few weeks earlier on our trip from Oregon to New Jersey. Perhaps I had a bit more travel experience than the average teenager, but compared to my fellow Olympians, I was an amateur.

Case in point: I had a middle seat on the flight. All the way in the back of the plane. Big mistake. I had not chosen this seat for myself; it was booked by USA Track and Field after the trials. I didn't know I could be more specific with my preference on a seat. The flight was miserable. I was crammed between strangers who spent the entire flight sneezing and coughing. It was like one of those movie scenes where you think, *That doesn't happen in real life*. I can confirm; it really does happen.

The day after we touched down in Rio, I had a fever and was feeling nauseous and congested. At the time, the Zika virus was all over the news. A few athletes considered not going because of the spread of the virus in Brazil. Out of an abundance of caution, several members of my family stayed home while Mom and Dad accompanied me to Brazil. Thankfully, I didn't have Zika. But I was diagnosed with a nasty cold when the medical team met me in the Olympic Village to check me over. Not an ideal way to kick off my Olympic experience.

The first few days were rougher than rough. With my immune system trying to fight the infection, I was exhausted all the time. I hardly left my room, which meant I didn't get the proper nutrition or the tour of the village to know where everything was. Since I was staying in the Olympic Village, thankfully there were doctors who could prescribe medicine and give me some snacks to keep me nourished.

My room was small. The mattress . . . let's just say Tempur-Pedic had a new customer when I got home. I slept on the ground toward the end of my time there. My roommate was Vashti Cunningham, an eighteen-year-old high jumper. The first five days I was in Rio, I didn't see much of her, or anyone else for that matter. The sickness kept me quarantined in my room. It wasn't that anyone told me to stay there; it was that I didn't have the energy even to get out of bed. All I had to eat was a snack basket

Team USA provided the athletes and a few meals my roommate dropped off for me. I spent most of each day sleeping, watching Netflix, texting friends, and, when I could, updating my parents on my health. I kept them in the loop, but I didn't give them specifics because I didn't want them to worry. They would have kicked into parent mode and made some heroic effort to help me. But as the new kid on the block, I tried to act as if I'd been there before. I pretended this cold was no big deal.

One thing I couldn't do was check social media. I'd deleted my accounts a few weeks before the Olympic trials. Throughout high school, I'd been active on social media, checking my Instagram account multiple times a day. I liked posting what I was doing and seeing what my friends were up to. But by the Olympic trials, I had deleted Instagram and Twitter after an incident earlier that year. What used to be a place where I connected with friends had become a source of turmoil.

It started the second semester of my junior year. I found out that the guy I was going out with at the time had cheated on me. After we broke up, the individual he cheated on me with sent me a message on Instagram. There was no apology. No, "Sorry about that. Things got out of hand. I know this must be tough for you." Instead, this person mocked me, made fun of me, and was about as cruel as one human being can be to another. Though I had been wronged, the antagonist made me out to be the bad guy. It seemed like every time I logged on to Instagram, there was a private message filled with all kinds of unkind, vicious, inappropriate, and awful comments. Not long after the trolling started, it became public. First there were comments made on social media, subtle shots at my character for the online world to see. Then it seemed like everyone in my school knew about the broken relationship. That betrayal became a topic for the entire school to whisper about in the hallways and gossip about in person and online. I couldn't make the drama go away entirely, but I could delete social media and at least not see it as much.

The decision to get off social media helped me avoid the drama and just generally be happier, so I'd stayed off it through the Olympics. Though it might have relieved some of the boredom to be able to scroll mindlessly through Instagram while I was cooped up in my tiny dorm room in the Olympic Village, I'm glad I didn't have Instagram when I was in Rio. If I had, I would have seen what people had to say about me—the good and the bad—and none of it would have helped my mental state.

After five long, boring days by myself—a now-seventeen-year-old in a foreign country with no family or friends around—I recovered enough to venture out of my room. There was so much to see. I hadn't yet been to any of the venues. I was just now getting to explore the Olympic Village. Rio was an exotic place, unlike anywhere I'd ever been. I wanted to get out and see it, but I couldn't stray too far from the village just yet.

So where was my first stop on my Olympic adventure? McDonald's.

I didn't just pass by McDonald's and grab an item or two. I kind of binged it. By day five, I needed food badly, and I didn't know where to get it. I was too nervous and shy to ask anyone for directions to the cafeteria or a semihealthy place where I could get a salad or sandwich. So in my angst and fear of sounding ridiculous, I set up shop at McDonald's. Athletes could get up to twenty items a day for free. Don't worry; I didn't max out that allotment. I would have looked very different stepping on the track if I had. Still, I ate lots of chicken nuggets. Fries. Hamburgers. Not exactly athlete fuel, but honestly, can you blame me? It was free food. Looking back, it wasn't my brightest moment, but I still had my teenager metabolism. That Olympic Village McDonald's seemed like it was built for me.

BACK ON THE TRACK

With only a couple of days left until my first qualifying heat, the quarterfinals, I made it out to the track for the first time, where my high school coach, Mike McCabe, and I were finally able to start training after my illness. We didn't work too hard. Since I was recovering from being sick, the goal was simply to get me outside and over a few hurdles.

I always had this sense that being in an Olympic race would somehow feel different. I'd never analyzed what that meant. I guess I just thought the spotlight was so big and the moment so extraordinary that it caused athletes to become the best possible version of themselves. I'd spent countless hours imagining the experience. With my up-and-down emotions and my fear of failure, I could see myself unable to get off the starting blocks, then running in slow motion in front of tens of thousands in the stadium and millions of TV viewers, gasping for breath as I came around the final turn or, worse, snagging a hurdle with my foot and crashing face-first into the track. Broken limbs, tears streaming down my face, just an absolute mess. The camera would zoom in on me, writhing in pain, the Olympic rings framing the bottom of the screen. My teenage imagination was something else.

Instead, the reality was much more ordinary. I didn't sleep great the night before the first qualifying heat in Rio, like any other race. I woke up several times, my leg twitching, my head spinning with images of the track. I hardly ate anything for breakfast (I took a break from the twenty-item menu at McDonald's for race day). And I dealt with that familiar pit in my stomach.

In warm-ups, the track felt like any other track. The stadium, while big, was not jammed with people. In fact, I remember being underwhelmed, and relieved, at the relatively small size of the crowd. And the competition? Well, I was so inside my own head, trying desperately to focus on the task at hand, that I didn't interact with any of them or, frankly, get a good look at any of the other world-class athletes. If I had paid more attention to who was beside me on the track that day, I'm sure I would have passed out.

Other than the World Youth Championships in Colombia the previous year, I hadn't yet competed internationally. Yet beside me there were grown women from Kenya, Cuba, Switzerland, Denmark, Italy, and the Czech Republic. Zuzana Hejnová from the Czech Republic was the most accomplished runner in my heat. I had watched her in previous years on TV in awe. She'd won the silver medal at the 2012 Olympics in London. She was also a two-time world champion in the 400-meter mark, winning the event in 2013, when I wasn't even in high school yet, and again in 2015. I was also matched up against Ristananna Bailey-Cole, one of Jamaica's fastest sprinters. Jamaica may be a tiny island nation, but in the world of track-and-field, it's a heavyweight, consistently producing some of the fastest men and women ever to compete.

Professionals like Zuzana and Ristananna had been preparing for this week every day since the end of the 2012 Olympics, when I was racing in a few local meets around New Jersey and thinking about what dress I was going to wear to my eighth-grade graduation. I genuinely thought I had no chance. I was trying to keep in mind what Dad had told me several times since I qualified for the team: "This is a good experience. Gets you used to the Olympics. There are no expectations on you." Sounded good.

When the announcer called for my fellow competitors and me to take our positions at the starting blocks, that familiar, always reliable instinct kicked in. It didn't matter how accomplished the other racers were, I was going to do everything I could to beat them.

The gun sounded, and as I took off down the track and cleared the first two hurdles, I actually thought, *Oh, this is just another race.* The track was the same. So were the hurdles. The competitors may have been older and more experienced, but that had no bearing on what happened in my lane. For the first 200 meters, I ran well, but I didn't run with any sense of desperation. This was a preliminary heat. The goal was qualifying for the next round, so, in a normal situation, most runners would hold back a little, try to conserve as much energy as possible. That was my strategy until I hit the 200-meter hurdle and realized that the Olympics was not, in fact, just another race. Though running well, I was lagging behind the leaders, closer to last than first. If I didn't pick up the pace, I wasn't going to qualify for the semi-finals. These women weren't just qualifying through the rounds; they were asserting their dominance. If I was going to make it to the next round, I couldn't hold anything back.

In countless races before, I'd find another gear down the homestretch. While others were tiring, I'd pick up enough speed to pass my competitors. I reached for that familiar kick as we worked for the finish line. Through the last 50 meters, I was sprinting, giving it everything I had. Yet I wasn't making up much ground, if any. I was stuck in the middle of the pack. I crossed the finish line in 56.32 seconds.

Did I qualify? The question repeated in my mind as I bent over, gasping for air, trying not to think about the fact that I'd just given a first heat more effort than expected. It seemed like a long shot that my Olympic racing would continue. There were six total heats. The top three finishers in each heat automatically qualified for the semifinals. I'd finished fifth in this one.

To keep racing, I'd have to have one of the next six fastest qualifying marks based on time, since I wasn't top three and automatically in. I was already behind Stina Troest of Denmark, who'd finished fourth in my heat. Chances were good another five women would best my time.

I vaguely recall keeping an eye on the remaining heats and my position in the standings, but I was too exhausted to care deeply. A first heat had never taken so much out of me. When I found out I'd made the semifinals later that day, I don't remember much of a reaction. Part of me was relieved. Exiting after the quarterfinals would have been embarrassing. Another part of me was dreading the next round. Partly because I was drained. Also because I was starting to hear the chatter surrounding my event.

At some point between the trials and the Olympics, the media started asking the question: *Could the female 400-meter hurdle podium be all Americans?* A New Jersey reporter—one who'd been following my career for several years—might have been the first to suggest an American sweep. He'd labeled me a child prodigy a few years back and tended to use quite a bit of hyperbole when describing my ability. To be honest, it freaked me out. I'd rather fly under the radar than get that kind of attention. With not much basis in reality, the media started to speculate that I'd win a medal alongside Dalilah Muhammad and Ashley Spencer. Other news outlets picked up on the idea, especially after all three of us made it through the first round. Then there was the success of the entire US Track and Field team in Rio, especially in hurdles. Our team swept the women's 100-meter hurdles, a first in Olympic history. Could lightning strike twice? If anyone knew just how hard I'd had to work to make it through the first round, they wouldn't have floated an all-American podium as a real possibility.

Alone in my dorm room back in the Olympic Village, I started to imagine the final. All the media attention. The crowds. The pomp and circumstance. If people were talking about an American sweep now, I assumed the speculation would reach a fever pitch if all three of us made the final. I knew if an American was going to fail to reach the podium, it was going to be me. Dalilah and Ashley were in the prime of their careers, both capable of winning gold. I wasn't. Also, I was fatigued. The travel, the uncomfortable bed, the cold, the first heat, not to mention the eight months of racing I'd already done that year, had left me physically and mentally spent.

As I went to bed that night, I didn't have a lot of confidence. I didn't believe I was going to do something special, fulfill my potential as a track-and-field "prodigy," as I'd often been called through the years. I thought the next day's race would be the final one of my Olympics, which would mercifully put an end to the American sweep talk. I wanted that to happen because I didn't understand that my identity shouldn't have been in whether I was measuring up to other people's expectations of me. My identity should have been in God, and I should have looked to him for meaning and purpose. But in 2016, I didn't know how to do that, so I felt hopeless when I was faced with a situation where I couldn't control what would happen and, for that reason, couldn't be sure how I would be perceived. And feeling so little control, the next day I would make a decision during that less-than-a-minute loop around the track in Rio that would, in a sense, forever shape me.

THE DECISION

The semifinals began like any other. On the starting blocks the instinct roared to life, cutting through the insecurity and nerves. It carried me to the 200-meter mark. Halfway through the race, I was running well, within striking distance of the final. But at some point over the next 100 meters, my instinct abandoned me, and I was left with just my thoughts. It was the first time it ever disappeared on the track. As I labored down the backstretch, leaping over hurdles when necessary, I suddenly found myself without the need, or even the desire, to win. I found myself actually formulating full sentences inside my head as I endured one of the most physically grueling minutes in sports. *It's been such a long season. I made it further than I thought I would. No one is going to be mad at me. Just be done.* And just like that, I threw the race.

I'm not proud of those thoughts. They weren't me. I'd always prided myself on my competitive nature, my will to win, my ability to push through difficult situations. A natural inclination. Now here I was, in the biggest moment of my racing life, arguably my entire life, and I wasn't just having those thoughts;

I was listening to them. Around the final turn, my patented final push to the finish line didn't show up. I didn't even try to find it. Instead, I slowed down just enough to make sure I wouldn't make it to the finals. I coasted to the finish line. Still, I have grace for young Sydney. She was absolutely terrified of what would come next. Without a sense of direction, her fight-or-flight kicked in, and to protect herself from harm, she let up on her speed.

I crossed the finish line in 56.22 seconds: fifth in my heat. More than a second behind the last qualifying time. As soon as the race was over, my inner voice practically screamed, *Yes! Your season is done!*

Even if I had given that race everything I had, my season might have still been done. One second is a lot of ground to make up in the 400-meter hurdles. Could I have snagged one of the last qualifying times if I'd wanted it desperately? I don't know. I'll never know. And it wasn't long after the race was over, and my body wasn't in pain anymore, that the uncertainty, that feeling of regret, began to take hold.

As soon as I got back to my temporary home in the Olympic Village, guilt began to rush upon me. I was such a competitor. Why, under any circumstances, would I slow down? What was causing that? Who cared if I didn't live up to the expectations of the media, fans, or anyone else? What about my high school coaches, who were also a part of this experience? Had I just robbed them of an opportunity of a lifetime as well?

Maybe perfectionism was telling me, *If I can't be perfect, why even try?* Of course, that's a dangerous mindset this side of heaven for all of us. We'll never be perfect here on earth. Though God made us to want to progress, to improve, to grow, he never promised us we'll be perfect. That was certainly true of

> Though God made us to want to progress, to improve, to grow, he never promised us we'll be perfect.

my running. It's also true for you no matter your job or calling in life. I was trapped in the perfectionism mindset back in 2016. It made me wonder what the point was if I couldn't be flawless on the track. That was certainly the wrong question, and it led to an unfortunate result.

A day or two later, I watched Ashley Spencer win bronze and Dalilah Muhammad bring home gold for the US in the final—finally getting the US its first gold in the 400-meter hurdles. I couldn't help but wonder if I could have joined them on that podium. I would have had to run the fastest race I'd ever run, but that time wasn't impossible, not during the Olympics. I left that event feeling like I had more to give but not knowing if I'd get the chance to give it. This opportunity wasn't guaranteed to come back to me again, and I had to live with my decisions. I hoped and prayed that one day, I would get the chance to end up on that podium, knowing that I gave it every ounce I had.

GOODBYE RIO

Despite the setbacks, I had to acknowledge that my family, coaches, and I were still living the dream of attending the Olympics. We had to make some time to enjoy it. With my event behind me, I felt free to just be a kid. I moved from the Olympic Village to the apartment where my parents were staying. We explored the city and attended as many events as we could, including diving and the 100-meter sprint, where Usain Bolt won yet another gold medal. I'll never forget the energy in the stadium that night: one of the greatest moments in Olympic history. I'm grateful I had the opportunity to be part of it.

Each day there were sweet moments, surprises that happen only at the Olympics. Spending time with my high school coaches truly made me feel less bad about my actions in the semifinal. Watching them get to experience this new adventure with me was an amazing moment none of us will ever forget. From the classroom to the world stage, we had accomplished far more than we imagined when our season began. Moments like these were truly memorable.

The highlight for me was the closing ceremonies. For any Olympic athlete, there's nothing cooler than strolling around a stadium, wearing your country's colors, surrounded by the world's greatest athletes. For those few moments, I felt like I belonged. I forgot all the fear and hardships that had been part of my Olympic journey. Maybe, I thought, it had all been worth it.

Still, the thought looming in the back of my mind was that I had some growing up to do. Maybe I had the physical gifts to reach the finals or possibly even win a medal in Rio, but I was not mentally prepared to do what it was going to take to maximize my ability. A deep-seated anxiety was gnawing at me, haunting my preparation and relationships, stealing rest and disrupting any semblance of peace. That's not a healthy way to live. It wasn't sustainable, and even back then I knew it. How could I manage coming back to the Olympic Games and having the correct mindset to be successful? I wanted to know how to manage these emotions. My desire to be Olympic champion was still there,

> In between my first and second Olympics, everything would change.

but at that point I thought it would take a miracle to achieve my dream.

From Eugene to Rio, the summer of 2016 showed me how much control my fear had over me. It dominated the track that summer. And after Rio, the fear didn't go away. It grew until it infected every part of my life.

I didn't know it then, but in between my first and second Olympics, everything would change. I would change. I'd become a different person. A new person. One filled with hope, joy, and faith. One ready to run the best race of my life. It wasn't an easy road. When I left Rio, I thought I was leaving behind the biggest challenge of my life. I had no idea that the next two years would be even harder. And to reach joy, I had to go through trials too big for me to face on my own.

Chapter 4

Of the 127 American track-and-field athletes who came home after the Olympics, I'm guessing I was the only one who enrolled in high school physics a few weeks later. I didn't have a guidebook for the transition from the center of the sports world to my senior year of high school. Only a few people had ever done it before. It wasn't easy.

Not long after the Olympics ended that year, Dunellen, the small New Jersey borough where I'd gone to elementary and middle school, hung signs around displaying this was my hometown. That included our local track. I was grateful for the recognition but also felt undeserving. Normally, people who receive this kind of honor have accomplished a lot. They're near the end of their career or retired. I had barely checked anything off my to-do list. I know my town was just excited for me, as well as proud, but the competitor within me felt even more obligated to hurry and achieve my goals to validate this gesture.

At the unveiling ceremony, I dropped the black cloth, revealing the sign with my name on it. Cameras snapped my photo. I knew I was supposed to smile and tell the reporters and the local politicians what an honor this was. How surreal it was to have a track where I used to run now showcase my name. And that's what I did. Still, it felt like a lot of adult responsibility. I was now a namesake of our one-square-mile town. I didn't quite know how to process it.

I was also taken aback by a documentary that was made about my life as both a high school senior and Olympian. Produced by FloTrack, a subscription video streaming service that covers elite runners, the short film followed me from class to class one day, culminating with an indoor training session (must have been raining the day they filmed) where we ran the halls of my high school. They interviewed me in the gym, asking me to talk about what kind of difference I wanted to make in the world and how I planned to influence a younger generation.[3] Everyone seemed to forget that I *was* the younger generation.

Inside, I felt like I still needed good role models to help me through all these wild changes, yet everyone was already looking at me differently, expecting me to share wisdom I did not yet possess. Of course, I would do my best, but I started to feel like I was coming to the end of my internal resources. I felt like the words I was sharing were what I assumed people wanted to hear. Much of it was advice I didn't even take for myself but was quick to give others. For the most part, it seemed to help and encourage people too. That surprised me, but I regret that it didn't always come from a genuine place. I can honestly say that my insight is now genuine, but at that time my goal was to make sure the image fit the expectation.

Then there were the requests for autographs and selfies. At first it was fun. Kids would stop me in the halls and ask to take a picture. People would want my signature at a meet. It was the kind of attention I couldn't help but enjoy. But there were moments when I felt uncomfortable, especially because I was so young and still trying to figure out who I was, what my calling in life would be, and what I believed. How was I to handle being viewed as a role model, with people considering me an inspiration, yet I didn't even know who I was? Every day was an internal battle to reconcile those two things. I'll never forget the girl who followed me into the bathroom at a meet, asked for a picture while I was in a stall, then waited for me to finish my business. When I finished and emerged, feeling embarrassed and uncomfortable, she pulled out her phone and we took the picture right there . . . still in the bathroom. (I washed my hands first, just for clarity.) I'm sure the photo showed up on social media not long after.

A week or two after the Olympics, I had jumped back on Instagram mostly because there were all these fake accounts popping up, claiming to be me. I didn't want to confuse anyone, so I made a new account just so people would know those other accounts weren't real. Days after I reacclimated to Instagram, I got messages from a plethora of professional athletes, entertainers, and musicians. Many of them were from men who were much older than I was, definitely not the kind of attention a senior in high school needed. Still, I am grateful for all those experiences. They forced me to grow up and adjust to having all of this attention at such a young age.

DIVIDING LINES

Coming back to high school was a difficult landscape to navigate. People were looking at me a certain way. There was an unspoken expectation to be a mature woman, yet I was still expected to finish my senior year, choose a college, go to prom, and continue being the same person I was before Rio. How in the world was I going to do that? Everything about my life was now different.

I understood the excitement and newness of all the endeavors that were coming my way, as well as to those around me. Still, the reality was, this wasn't normal. For example, my school gained much notoriety from the 2016 Olympic Games, as did our track team. We were now viewed in an even bigger spotlight with expectations and curiosity for what we were going to do next. Everything was heightened. But is that really what teenagers need? More eyes on them, more love, and even more hate? The short answer is no, but in reality, there was no choice. I was now navigating the jungle of senior year.

A month into school, I started getting the feeling that some of my peers were not too fond of the changes. What had started off as an exciting, hopeful year quickly turned into high school drama. Looking back, I must ask, did I bring it upon myself? Was I truly different than when I had left? Or were there hints of comparison that are so common among hormonal teenage girls? I don't know if I'll ever truly have a clear answer; I think it was a combination of both those things. Nonetheless, at the time, it felt like life-and-death. Wanting to be accepted by your peers and respected by your classmates is an major part of growing as a teenage girl. At a time when your body is changing, your life is shifting, and you're beginning to step into adulthood, you seek validation, especially from those closest to you. When I felt as though most people close to me now looked at me differently, I took it personally. Especially because some of those issues came even to the track, running became a burden, not the outlet it had previously been for me: a place to take a break from the grind of school and the ups and downs of relationships.

The adolescent pettiness became so frustrating that I seriously considered not running my senior year: quitting the Union Catholic track team and preparing for college on my own. Looking back, I don't think the issues that took place warranted such a drastic response, but I didn't have a better way to deal with them. I began dreading going to school because I didn't know what the day would bring. While I didn't quit the team, I did at one point reach my limit on what I could handle.

After talking with my coach multiple times, as well as with one of my closest friends and my parents, I decided I needed a solution. I began seeking counsel from a therapist to talk through my problems. I met with her once or twice a week, and we would discuss that week's ordeal, the role that I played, and how it made me feel, but never how I could confront these problems to bring reconciliation. I don't feel like I truly got the solution I was looking for, but I did get an outlet. Someone to talk to. I think that's what I was missing at that time. I wish I had known to go to God back then, because I know he would have heard my cries and prayers for help. His Word would have also given insight into

> I wish I had known to go to God back then, because I know he would have heard my cries and prayers for help.

55

helpful ways to approach broken relationships and be a peace-maker in the midst of trials.

The teenage drama continued for most of the year. During most practices, there was exclusion, whispering, jokes, and at times rude comments. I've never been one for confrontation, but I've also never been one for disrespect. So, in my frustration as the year came to a close, I made a drastic decision at the national meet.

It was the last meet of my senior year. It was a relay race, and I was asked to run the shuttle hurdles for a shot at winning a national title. That was my breaking point. I snapped. I told coach I wouldn't do it. He looked at me incredulously. "Sydney, it's a national title." But I didn't care. I sat out the race, forfeiting a national title for myself and the other girls. I just didn't see how we could call ourselves teammates and accomplish something together after how the year had gone. I knew they didn't like me; that was clear. But I also had resentment in my heart. And I didn't want to give them the satisfaction of winning when I was still hurt. They ended up not winning the race, and even though part of me felt justified, it didn't mend the broken relationships.

I know I didn't handle my return from Rio and my senior year at Union Catholic perfectly. There were a couple of reasons for that. First, I think there's something in all of us that thinks we can't build ourselves up unless we tear others down. After the Olympics, I was placed on a pedestal. Whenever we'd walk into a track meet, there was no lack of attention. Even before races would begin, I'd hear comments: "Look, it's Sydney McLaughlin." That was a big shift from before Rio, when no one knew who I was. They might comment on my speed after a race. But now, it seemed like everyone knew who I was before I started warming up. Pointing and snapping photos. No teenager should have that much attention on them. The pedestal isn't natural. It's a recipe for pride and relationship issues. And I think the pedestal was a big reason my teammates and I didn't get along my senior year. What they didn't know was that I would have gladly exchanged it all—all the attention, all the buzz—for better friendships on my team and at my school. I would often think back to my freshman year when everyone on the team truly loved each other. The support, camaraderie, and desire to win built an atmosphere that was unmatched. I desired nothing more than to feel that way again.

Second, there was a big difference in how I viewed my senior year of track and how the rest of the team saw it. For me, it was a stepping stone to a career. My plan was to make my last year of high school another stop on the road to some of the biggest races in the world, including the next Olympics in 2020. For the rest of the team, that senior year of high school wasn't a pit stop; it was the destination. Competing against the best high school teams in the state, and even the country, was going to be the high point of their career in track. Many of them were continuing to work toward getting scholarships, making their collegiate track teams, and securing a place for their futures. Perhaps that fact alone was part of what drove a wedge between us that year. I could see how, for some, it brought enmity between us. It also made me fundamentally different, isolated, and, at times, lonely. And that made it even harder than it already was to open up to others, trust them, and build lasting relationships.

Similar drama marked my time at church that year. When I was growing up, my family attended church every Sunday. Church was a part of my life, no different than going to school, and no different than going to practice. I knew it was Sunday's activity. Worship was my favorite time; I loved to sing the songs, even though the messages flew right by my head. Most of the time I would sit in church texting, drawing, or daydreaming about what was about to take place at school on Monday. Still, church had always been a refuge for me, a place to step away from the repetitive rigors of life for a few hours. That changed my senior year. What used to feel like a place of acceptance became a place of angst.

During my high school years, much of my church friend group began giving their lives to Christ, which means they confessed him as Lord, repented of their sins, and were baptized in the name of Jesus, symbolizing their devotion to a life that glorifies and honors him. Not wanting to be left behind, I began taking the steps that I was told would lead me to the same place. During this process, I realized just how much I wasn't doing this for the right reasons. I didn't understand what I was being taught or feel convicted in my heart that I truly wanted to follow God. I simply wanted to follow my friends. With that, I decided I wasn't ready and stopped my spiritual journey.

One girl I had been very close with for years had fully devoted herself to God, and with that brought change. Many of our conversations beforehand had been about boys, dancing, and jokes. Now I began to see the difference in our friendship. Much of what had been leisurely conversation shifted to questions pertaining to where my faith stood. Things such as, *did I love track more than God? Was the boy I was dating a Christian? What if, after my races, I shared scriptures with the announcer?* All of those things sounded bizarre to me at the time.

I couldn't understand why she cared so much. As the tone of

our conversations changed, I was uncomfortable having them. I started to steer clear of her, wanting to avoid any uncomfortable interrogations. I didn't feel comfortable sharing these personal tidbits with her, mainly because I expected them to be met with disapproval. Looking back, it was a fear of judgment that drew me away from answering those questions. Her intention was to help draw me closer to God, but the last thing I wanted that year was more people in my business. (While this created distance in our friendship at that time, we did eventually reconcile as we matured.)

The opinions, comments, and continuous questions drove a wedge into our friendship, and as a result, my group of friends slowly whittled down to just me, myself, and I.

Those relationship problems translated into a new kind of fear: fear of being misunderstood or misjudged. That made me close my heart to others. During that time of life, nothing bothered me more than people viewing me in a way I didn't believe was true. When that happened, I was quick to cut off the relationship or end the friendship.

As I struggled to develop close relationships with people, my anxiety spread from the track, where I was terrified of losing, to relationships, where I became afraid of betrayal by those closest to me. And it made me eager for the fresh start of college, far from Union Catholic and Dunellen, New Jersey. If I couldn't handle the fear, I at least wanted a chance to run from it.

> Those relationship problems translated into a new kind of fear: fear of being misunderstood or misjudged.

A CHANGE OF SCENERY

Shortly before my last season of track at Union Catholic began, I had to make one of the biggest decisions of my life: Which college was I going to attend? Though there was plenty of speculation about whether I would go to college or turn pro right after high school, I never seriously considered skipping college. My parents, especially Mom, wouldn't let me think about it. I considered the Universities of Oregon, Texas, and Florida. All three have top-notch track-and-field programs. But I seriously scouted out only two schools: the University of Southern California (USC) and the University of Kentucky (UK).

From the start, USC was the front-runner. I'd loved the idea of Los Angeles since visiting the city for the first time in 2014. The seemingly endless sunshine. The beaches. The diversity, culture, and food appealed to me. So did the school itself. Alongside the beautiful campus, USC had one of the best communication programs in the world. Since that was my preferred major, it was the academic program I most wanted to be part of. On the track, I'd be learning from hurdles coach Joanna Hayes, who'd won gold in the 100-meter hurdles at the 2004 Olympic Games in Athens, Greece. The coaching staff and I truly bonded on that trip, and it just felt comfortable for me to be there. I remember standing on the track during my visit and saying to myself, "Man, this is it." With the mix of academic programs, a location in the heart of LA, and a high-caliber track-and-field team, I was sure I'd pick USC after my visit.

Next, I toured the University of Kentucky. What was the most memorable part of that visit? Coach Edrick Floréal.

At the end of my visit to UK's campus, Coach Flo, as everyone at Kentucky called him, was driving me around Lexington, pointing out landmarks and talking about my future. At that time, I still hadn't made up my mind. Coach Flo knew that, so he didn't try to convince me by trying to sell how enjoyable my college experience would be at UK. Instead, he said exactly what a driven, up-and-coming athlete wanted to hear.

"Sydney, where do you see yourself in five years?" he asked as he navigated us through downtown Lexington.

"I want to be an Olympic champion," I said. "And have the world record [in the 400-meter hurdles]."

I didn't lack for ambition, that was for sure. Other than that brief moment in Rio when I wanted the race to be over, I'd never had to force myself to compete. It was there before Rio. It roared back right after the Olympics. Being competitive was just part of how God hardwired me. I didn't have to push myself to think big when Coach Flo asked me that question. It was part of what made me Sydney.

Without hesitating, Coach Flo said, "We can do that." Then he listed the successful athletes he had coached, including Olympic champions, world champions, and world record holders. In that moment, I knew this place would challenge me. I wanted to be among the best, training for the best. Flashes of my future came into my mind, seeing myself with the gold medal around my neck at the Tokyo Olympics. Was this the best place to prepare for that? Coach Flo had confidence that it was. For me, that was enough.

I believed Coach Flo because he didn't tell me only what I wanted to hear. He also made it clear that if I came to Kentucky, he was going to completely overhaul my hurdles technique. He didn't sugarcoat what he thought of my current approach.

"It definitely needs some work, but we can fix it," he said. "You're jumping too high when you reach the hurdle. The less time you're in the air, the better."

According to Coach Flo, just about every part of my form was off. I kicked my trail leg too high in the air. The half step I'd often take just before a hurdle was too long and would slow me down. I depended too much on raw speed and competitive will. He was going to change that.

Coach Flo didn't just talk a big game. He had the results to back it up. Since becoming Kentucky's track-and-field coach in 2012, he'd built the school into one of the top programs in the country. He recruited top-level talent and transformed them into national champions. Under his tutelage, five women had won a combined seven individual national championships. In 2015, Kentucky finished second in the team competition. Along with the undergraduates he trained, he also worked with a stable of professional athletes. He specialized in coaching hurdlers. One of them was Kori Carter—a fellow competitor in the 2016 Olympic trials. Others were Keni Harrison and Omar McLeod, two of America's fastest sprinters. There was a reason they called it "Hurdle U" (Hurdle University).

These professionals trained at UK with the track-and-field team. That meant I would be training alongside the best athletes in the world on the Kentucky campus. I knew I needed that kind of accountability and day-in, day-out competition if I was going to achieve my goals.

When it was time to sign my national letter of intent, a contract that says I'm legally obligated to run on the track team of the school I've just signed with, I wanted to pick USC for the location, education, and opportunities I thought would be available living in LA. But I chose the University of Kentucky because of Coach Flo. I was sure he could take my career where I wanted it to go.

It seemed like Coach Flo and I were on the same page. Every interaction I'd had with him had seemed honest, straightforward, and full of optimism, energy, and positivity. He seemed to me almost like a father figure, someone I was sure I'd come to love and appreciate in the coming years. And during my last semester of high school, in the thick of the drama with my track teammates at Union Catholic High School, he was someone I turned to for support and guidance. I'd text and call him, asking questions about my training, about life at Kentucky, about what I could expect when I moved to Lexington. He was there for me at that time, someone I could talk to when I couldn't talk to my peers. Those conversations gave me something to look forward to, a change of scenery I could daydream about, a future I could escape to when high school was at its worst.

Brush it off, I told myself countless times when those last pre-graduation problems came around. *You'll be in college in just a few short months, and everything will be better.* Except, it wasn't.

TAKING THE FIGHT TO KENTUCKY

My second week into officially being a UK Wildcat, a fight broke out during a team meeting. I'd never seen two people attack each other, hit, claw, scratch, scream, and swear before my eyes. I'd seen plenty of arguments between teammates. I'd endured some myself. But this was on a different level.

I don't remember the exact reason for the fight. The girls used to be friends. So I was very confused as to what was happening. It started off as a conversation to try to clear things up, then escalated into some yelling, and then the next thing I knew, they were brawling.

It made me sick to my stomach, not just because it was the first time I'd watched a disagreement turn violent but also because it shattered my innocent belief that the kind of drama I'd seen in high school wouldn't happen in college. I'd assumed that during this new life stage I'd be surrounded by mature people, individuals who weren't interested in drama. I seriously don't know what I was thinking. I must have believed I was moving to Mars. It was becoming more and more clear that no matter where I went, I wasn't going to escape conflict. I couldn't run from it. People were still going to be people. Words still hurt, feelings still existed, and problems still arose. I came to the realization that college wasn't going to solve all of my problems, so when I found myself right back in the same old drama as high school, I almost packed my bags and left.

I nearly ran from the team room after watching that fight, and I called my dad.

"I made a huge mistake," I blurted out when he picked up the phone. "I don't know what I'm doing here. I should have gone to USC."

As he did at the 2016 Olympic trials, my dad calmed me down. Encouraged me to stick it out. Reminded me of what we'd decided before I began college. I'd go for a year or two and then leave school and start my career on the track. I was there to learn from Coach Flo, improve my technique, get an education, then turn pro. No matter how bad I thought it was, I couldn't drop out after the second week. Bummer.

Though I'm glad I didn't quit after the fight, I can't say that college got any easier. In a lot of ways, that year was the hardest year yet.

First, there was the injury. About halfway through my first season at Kentucky, I started to notice a sharp pain in my right foot. I'm not sure exactly what I was doing when it happened, but I do know that my shoes either caused the injury or made it worse.

Since I was younger, I'd always worn New Balance shoes. They fit me perfectly and kept my feet—my most valuable asset—free from injury. Having quality shoes is crucial, and where many high school athletes were beginning to experience the traumas of injury, New Balance shoes kept me running on cloud nine.

At Kentucky, I couldn't wear New Balance. The team had an equipment deal with another company, so I had to wear their shoes. The unfamiliar feel, combined with the relentless training routine—and I mean absolutely relentless—started to wear down my foot. I complained about it to the coach and told him my foot didn't feel right. I felt like he didn't take my complaint seriously, even though the injury only continued to get worse. Yet I did what I was told. It never caused me to miss a race, but it ended up being a stress fracture that I would not find out I had until a year later.

Training was the second reason the 2017–18 school year was the hardest yet. It was grueling. I felt like I had no idea what it meant to even really run until I came to Kentucky.

With Coach Flo, there were no days off. We had to be in the weight room multiple mornings a week by 6 or 7 a.m. (a brutal wake-up call for any college kid). I had lifted some weights in high school, but with little strategy and less know-how. In college, those daily weight-room sessions were fully monitored by strength coaches. They pushed me harder than I'd ever been pushed, until my body was burned out and exhausted. From the weight room we'd head to class, then a few hours later to the track, where I would run until my body was begging to stop.

Mondays were the worst. That was the day we would run to a different stratosphere. Coach would make us run the longest distances I'd ever run in my life. I truly dreaded Monday's practice because I knew we would be going around and around and around. On Tuesdays, we'd focus on technique and form. Wednesdays were for strengthening our core and increasing our mobility. Thursdays were like Tuesdays. On Fridays, Coach would make us sprint until we couldn't breathe, with more speed and endurance training. Saturday was no time for rest or recreation. It was another day of sprints and hurdles. Sunday mornings we had to report to the team room at 10 a.m. for body treatment. Stretching, icing, massages, ice baths, whatever you needed, this was the time specifically designed for everyone to check in with the team's medical staff. To this day, I wish I'd pushed back, insisted on going to church instead of Sunday treatment. I can't help but wonder what the response would have been. I had found a church in Lexington that reminded me of the one I attended back home. A nice family was willing to pick me up each week. They'd even invited me to their house for dinner. Yet when the season truly picked up because of travel or treatment, I never went back. I wonder how much mental relief it would have brought me had I gone and found true treatment and rest for my heart and soul.

My relationship with Coach was the third and final reason that year at Kentucky was the hardest of my life. Don't get me wrong; he did a lot of great things for me. He definitely made me tougher. He taught me how to run the hurdles the right way. He turned me from a prodigy with poor technique to a disciplined, focused competitor ready for the professional circuit. But the expectations that were placed on me at just eighteen years old often made me wonder if he truly understood the weight of his expectations.

Several times I was called to his office, I assumed to talk about my performance on the track. That wasn't the case.

"What were you doing hanging around that basketball player?" he asked me once, a curious tone in his voice. "What's going on with you two?"

I was stunned. I had no idea how Coach knew about that relationship. And it was hardly a relationship. We were friends from before orientation who connected on Instagram when we both learned we were going to the school. Definitely not boyfriend and girlfriend. Literally just friends. I had only seen him once or twice around campus, yet Coach knew. I was surprised by that. I guess his intention was possibly to keep me from distractions, but it still felt like another barrier placed in front of me.

It made me feel on edge about where I was going, what I was doing, and who I was talking to. One Saturday, Coach called me around 7 or 8 p.m. to tell me that I had to "get it together," that I needed to reach 52 seconds in the 400-meter hurdles and less than 50 seconds in the open 400-meters, to lead our team to a national championship. Never mind that no one had ever run some of those times at the collegiate level. It left me wracked with anxiety. At this point, I truly felt I was giving all that I had, physically, mentally, and emotionally. How was I supposed to lead our team to a championship as a freshman? How was I going to run a sub-50-second 400-meter race given the fact that my foot felt like it was going to fall off? I couldn't relax. Every day the expectations required of me felt beyond my reach.

The year was exhausting. I gave everything I had to the sport, to my peers, and to myself. Yet I was miserable. My high hopes of coming to a place where I thought I would flourish quickly turned into a nightmare. At a routine medical checkup for athletes, I was even diagnosed with mild depression. It was comforting to know that what I was feeling was valid. I was a little depressed.

I saw so clearly at this time my need for God. There were days where I would just sit on my dorm bed looking at a Bible, not knowing what I was reading. I was searching for any sort of comfort or solace. It never came. Not because God wasn't there but because I wasn't truly seeking him. I was seeking a Band-Aid, something to cover the pain, something to pass the time just to get me to the next thing planned. That's not how God works, though, as I would learn in years to come.

Near the end of our season, I started to hear rumors that Coach was going to take a coaching job at the University of Texas. I didn't think the rumors were serious, but if they were, I was planning to go with him because I had seen results in my hurdle form as well as my sprint mechanics. My desire to be the best athlete in the world overshadowed my desire to be in a healthy environment. But after speaking with my parents and some of my closest friends, they encouraged me to go a different direction. They'd seen what I'd been going through and told me it was okay if I didn't run as fast if it meant I'd be happy. With everything I'd been facing, that felt like a relief. There was a different possibility for me than more of the same.

Days before US Nationals, Coach called me. "We're going to Texas," he announced in the most matter-of-fact way. I guess the rumors were true.

By that point, I'd made up my mind: I was not going with him. I opted instead to end my time at college and go professional. It was a big step. There were so many reasons that turning professional was the right decision for me. With my parents' and friends' support, I was ready to turn over a new leaf.

Despite all the growing pains and disappointments, though, that year in Kentucky was not a waste. There is much about my freshman experience I will always be grateful for. I did make lifelong friends I still talk to today. Much of the supporting staff truly became like family to me during many of my trials. They were constant encouragers throughout the grueling season. I had roommates for the first time in my life, friends who helped take away the loneliness and boredom that so often comes when you're traveling from race to race. I met some very special people there.

Some of Coach's strategies did produce results that couldn't be denied—I had a strong year on the track: setting the world junior 400-meter record when I clocked 50.36 at the SEC Championships. And I'll always cherish the national title I won in the 400-meter hurdles. Still, to this day, I struggle to trust people in part because of what happened in college. As a result, when someone wants to befriend me, an old fear can raise its head. I can't help but wonder, *What do you want? What's in it for you?* The wall that came with those questions, that made me fear people and struggle to cultivate genuine relationships, thickened

> When we allow life's concerns to cause us to build up walls from the outside world, we can become trapped in isolated rooms of our own building.

during my only year in college. Fear does that. When we allow life's concerns to cause us to build up walls from the outside world, we can become trapped in isolated rooms of our own building.

Despite the trials, I was excited and eager as I packed my bags and drove back to New Jersey in June 2018. The professional world was opening to me. My life was about to change in monumental ways. What those were, I didn't yet know.

Chapter 5

Up to this point in my life, nearly every decision besides college was made for me. As a young girl, I didn't often get to pick what I ate for dinner. If I had, I would have eaten a lot more McDonald's. When I was a teenager, my parents decided if we had the money for the new clothes and jewelry I wanted. My bedtime. My whereabouts. My weekend plans. I was accountable to someone for all of it. I was used to asking permission. Yet as soon as I turned professional, I was faced with the most crucial decision a professional runner can make.

My parents and agents could provide insight and counsel, but only I could decide which shoe brand I'd represent. The wrong choice could do a lot of harm, especially since I was recovering from an injury in college. Most people work with their hands. I work with my feet. These were my moneymakers, so this decision weighed heavily on me from the moment I turned professional.

Another reason picking the correct shoe company is important is because the company becomes your partner. How your contract is structured, the people you will interact with, and how much they want to involve you in their brand all play a part in an athlete's career. So I wasn't just picking my shoes; I was picking a team. Who was going to support me in both good and bad times, whether I was winning or losing? Would I have freedom to create my own shoes or clothing? Was I truly going to feel valued and wanted, or was I going to simply be another athlete? I was determined to make sure I made the right choice. The irony is, I almost screwed it up.

THE RIGHT FIT

Before any shoe decisions could be made, the first step in becoming a professional track-and-field athlete was choosing an agent. This individual would help me enter meets, negotiate appearance fees, and handle travel. Thankfully, this choice was not hard at all. During my one year at Kentucky, collegiate athletes were not allowed to have conversations with agents. Eligibility rules were very strict, and as a result, my parents ended up weeding out most of my options. Once I declared I was going professional, all I had to do was choose from the three options they had already preselected. I trusted my parents' judgment; they had looked out for me my entire life, and I knew if they were bringing these people in front of me, they trusted I would be in good hands.

Also, my parents were not easily fooled. They asked the hard questions, did the research, and did not take any gifts from anyone. They were so strict about this that they went as far as to bring their own water bottles to the meetings so there would be no confusion about whether I'd received anything before I officially turned pro. Their preparation and teamwork are a big reason for my success today. My parents ensured I would be in the best situation possible, especially being an eighteen-year-old about to accumulate a whole lot of money. Trust and integrity are everything, and my parents wanted to ensure I wouldn't get taken advantage of. So it only made sense to go with Wes Felix (the older brother of Allyson Felix) who I believed would be a great representative for me. Along with Wes came the amazing opportunity to work in conjunction with William Morris Endeavor, one of the world's largest, most reputable talent agencies. With Wes and my commercial agent Rob on my side, the possibilities seemed limitless.

In August, my new track agent set up meetings in New York City with four major shoe companies. Over the course of a few days, he, my mom and dad, and I met with Nike, Adidas, Under Armour, and New Balance. In each presentation, the company talked about why I would be a good fit for their brand. They brought free products, showed me PowerPoint presentations, and filled the room with whatever they thought would get my attention—namely, candy and sunflowers. They did their research. Following these meetings, each offered me an endorsement deal. I'd wear their shoes, uniforms, and apparel exclusively. All other sportswear brands would be out of the picture. If I decided to be their brand ambassador, they'd pay me a yearly salary.

Nike is the biggest brand in my sport. Long before they sold basketball shoes, or anything else really, they had a corner on the running market. Some of the biggest names in the sport—including Allyson Felix and Sanya Richards-Ross—had deals with Nike. Adidas is the second largest in the track space. Both promised me great contracts, lots of exposure, and shoes fitted to my feet. Yet after meeting with Under Armour and New Balance, I knew I'd eventually go with one of those two brands.

New Balance was the obvious choice. I couldn't remember a time when I hadn't worn their shoes. After suffering the stress fracture in college, a return to New Balance would have kept the problem from getting worse. They had been like family to me since I was a freshman in high school: making our high school team custom uniforms, inviting our team to hospitality events, and even asking me to participate in a world-record distance medley attempt my senior year after Rio. The meeting began with a highlight video of all my successes since the beginning of freshman year. My greatest feats were part of an epic reel, every scene flashing the logo *NB*. There were discussions about making me a face-of-the-brand athlete, giving me my own athleisure line. They even brought custom spikes with my name on them. So naturally, you would think I knew without a doubt what decision I was going to make. Normally, I am a very predictable, calculated person. I don't tend to stray too far from the safest option. This, though, was not one of those times.

There was something intriguing about Under Armour. They brought three large vision boards filled with their plans to make me the face of their track-and-field division, which at the time wasn't big. They said the possibilities were endless. We could build the brand together. As I listened, I wondered if this would be my chance to make a name for myself. My concept of image started to hold more sway in the decision than common sense.

A few days after we'd talked with each of the four brands, my agent Rob called. He informed me that New Balance and Under Armour had both given offers. My parents and I briefly discussed our thoughts about the meetings and felt confident we knew what was going to take place. What I didn't know at the time was that they and I were thinking about different brands. After much deliberation and thought, I had made up my mind: I was going with Under Armour. I was excited. I had this image in my head of myself on posters—the face of track-and-field for this hip, new brand in the sport. To make it official, they just needed my signature. Before the paperwork reached me and I became irrevocably a part of Under Armour, my mom sat me down to talk about the decision I'd just made.

The conversation happened at Dunkin' Donuts. I'll never forget it, partially because it would turn out to be such a pivotal conversation but also because it wasn't like my mom to even have this kind of conversation. Since I'd turned professional, she and my dad had decided to leave all the big decisions up to me. After their help finding my agent, they agreed not to try to manage or control my fledgling career. So when she pushed back against a decision I'd made, I knew I should listen.

"I have to be honest with you, honey, I think you made the wrong choice going with Under Armour."

I was stunned. Mom and Dad had listened quietly as each company made its pitch. They hadn't tried to push me one way or the other. Now that the decision was all but made, Mom was stepping in. Seeing as how I had just let the New Balance offer run out of time, I was terrified as she continued speaking.

"New Balance has treated you like family since you were fourteen years old," she continued. "They've always taken care of you. Their shoes work for you. The overall success rate you would have with them is better than with a company that might not be able to get the shoes right."

I immediately knew she was right. My feet were my greatest asset. Why would I go with a company that had no proof it would be a good match? I had made my decision based on feelings and image, but it lacked perspective. I wasn't investing in my future. Later that day, Dad told me he agreed with Mom (no surprise there).

I called my agent and told him I'd made a mistake. I wanted to go with New Balance if they'd still have me. It was a nerve-racking day or two as I waited for their response. After Mom shook me out of my youthful vanity, I had become terrified that I'd made a potentially career-altering decision that would haunt me for years to come. Thankfully, when my agent called back, he had good news: New Balance was willing to renegotiate our expired offer. *Thank God*, I remember thinking as my agent talked about the deal. Their kindness and patience confirmed that I'd made the right decision. I've been with New Balance my entire career and have yet to second-guess a thing.

THE RIGHT COACH

Alongside signing with New Balance, the other big decision I had to make that summer was who was going to coach me. Coach Flo wanted me to follow him to Texas. I knew that was out of the question. Instead, what I wanted was a fresh start. A new coach.

New city. New perspective on life and track. I found all that in Los Angeles and under the watchful eye of Joanna Hayes, the coach I'd thought about signing with at USC.

Joanna was a track legend in her own right. At the 2004 Summer Olympics in Athens, she'd won gold in the 100-meter hurdles. I'd met her during my recruitment visit at USC. At the time, working with her had been appealing to me. It was the main reason I wanted to go to USC. In order to take me on as an athlete, Joanna stepped away from her position as the hurdle coach for the Trojans to train me full time. Now that I'd turned pro, training with her in Los Angeles seemed like the best and, frankly, most enjoyable option. So I was beyond grateful when she agreed to the proposal, and just like that, I shipped everything I owned out west. It wasn't just one plane ticket I was buying, though; my mother made the move with me. Seeing as how I didn't drive, was only nineteen years old, and had just come into a significant amount of money, there was simply no way I was moving across the country alone.

To help with the transition to Los Angeles and make sure I settled into my professional career, my mom left her job at Rutgers University and moved with me to LA. We settled into a two-bedroom apartment and started to figure out how to be roommates. Although that was a tough decision for my parents at the time, to be across the country from each other, their sacrifice allowed them to be present where they were needed most. My father stayed in New Jersey, where my younger brother Ryan was finishing his senior year of high school, while Mom and I moved to LA to settle into a new chapter in life. We were like two kids on vacation. We went to the beach. Checked off some tourist attractions. Bought my mom a new car. I don't know if life has ever been as full of possibility as it was in Fall 2018. Everything was new. The Southern California sun was new to me, and it never went away. The daily routine was new: no schoolwork, no team meetings. Nothing but training and spending that New Balance paycheck.

Each day, I'd go to the UCLA track, and Joanna and I would train with a simple goal in mind: win the World Championships. That was all I thought about at the end of 2018 and the beginning of 2019. But it wasn't going to be easy to do. Dalilah wasn't just the top-rated female in the 400-meter hurdles; she was arguably one of the greatest of all time. I knew what it would take to compete with her: a new personal best.

At the beginning of 2019, the 400-meter world record holder was Russian Yuliya Pechonkina. She ran it in 52.34 seconds on August 8, 2003. Sixteen years later, her record was still standing. That's an eternity on the track, where athletes are always figuring out how to run faster than the previous generation. When I began my professional career, that record seemed a little too far out of reach. The real question for 2019 was, who would win the world championship: me or Dalilah? Seeing that this was only my first season as a pro, and it was her sixth season, I did not have the upper hand. Still, I was willing to try.

FACING THE COMPETITION

I knew there were two places where Dalilah and I would clash head-to-head for important titles. The first would be at the US National Track and Field Championships. This was to qualify us for the major meet of the season, which was the World

Championships in Doha, Qatar, in October 2019, a year after I turned professional and moved to Los Angeles. From the moment I became a professional, I had my sights set on those two events. Every track-and-field athlete lines up their season to peak for these two moments. If I didn't win anything else that year, my season would be a success if I took the titles at the US Nationals and Worlds.

My first race as a professional had been in Boston in January 2019, an open 500-meter, not the 400-meter hurdles I specialized in. New Balance organized the meet. It was an enjoyable yet unrealistic introduction to professional racing. Walking away with the win helped boost my confidence heading into the rest of the season. But the reality of the pro circuit hit me a few months later when I ran what, to this day, is one of the most difficult, and strangest, events of my life: a Diamond League race in Shanghai, China.

Track competitions are broken down into what I like to call tiers. Based on their level of importance and difficulty, a track athlete can decide which meets make sense for certain parts of the season depending on the overall goal. The top would be the Olympic Games, which, as most people know, takes place every four years. This is the cream of the crop when it comes to a track athlete's career. This is the moment we all dream and pray for since we were kids—wearing that Olympic medal around our necks while our national anthem plays. Next is the World Championships. They take place every other year, bordering the Olympics, pre- and post-. Like in the Olympics, athletes represent their home country competing for world titles. After that comes the Diamond League circuit. These meets take place throughout the season in countries all over the world. Athletes compete for points depending on what place they take, which accumulate to make up what is called the Diamond League Final. The top eight in each event at the end of the season compete for the Diamond League trophy. This circuit takes place every year, so athletes can decide which events they want to compete in for tune-ups pre- or post-Olympics or Worlds. Then you have local meets, found in your city or state, that are good for more tune-ups heading into the more intense latter part of the season.

That's why I went to the Diamond League event in Shanghai. I'd never been to China before, and my body didn't adjust well to the long flight and unique food. I'd lost five pounds by the end of the trip, which was unhealthy in more ways than one.

This Shanghai event was an open 400-meters. No hurdles. It started at 4 a.m. Los Angeles time. I remember chugging coffee minutes before the race, and I almost ran into a woman from being so exhausted. I'd never done that before. Can't imagine I'll ever do it again. I remember yawning while I warmed up and thinking, *I might actually fall asleep while I run.*

When the gun sounded, I felt like I was running on sand. My legs felt like bricks. My arms felt like rubber bands. I didn't settle into the race and start to run like I was capable of until the 200-meter mark, halfway to the finish line. By that point I was too far back to catch the leader. I managed to make up some time down the homestretch, laboring across the finish line in second place. It was quite an introduction to the professional life. I learned a lot during that trip about what to expect on the international circuit, which I still hold firm to this day. First, bring your own food. Other countries have their customs and normal diets; your stomach may not always agree. Nor your taste buds. So bringing my own snacks and food became a must. Second, my body needed more time to adjust to the time change, more sleep than I had received, and more nutrients than I was feeding it.

As the season progressed, I became more and more comfortable with each race until I finally had the chance to put my mark on the professional scene in June. I traveled to Oslo, Norway, for another Diamond League event. This was a 400-meter hurdles with star power. Dalilah was there, as were some of my other most talented competitors. All the prerace hype was focused on the two of us. She was the current Olympic champion, number one in the world. I was the up-and-comer, nearly ten years her junior.

I was patient that day. Dalilah is a pacesetter. From the starting blocks, she moved out front and pushed the field. I took the opposite approach. I stayed behind, keeping the leaders within striking distance, and relied on a big kick at the end—not by choice but because I had smashed the first hurdle with my trail leg and nearly wiped out. I fell behind by a lot that day, but I came roaring back over the final 100 meters, roaring past several racers, including Dalilah, to take first place. Crouching just past the finish line, gasping for breath, I remember thinking, *Oh, maybe she's not as scary as I thought. This isn't too bad.*

It was clear, even moments after the race, that Dalilah was not happy. After Oslo, she disappeared, and I didn't hear any news of her or her coach until the US Nationals the next month. I'd find out later that she doubled down on her training, pushing herself to the limits, determined to do whatever it took to ensure she wouldn't have a repeat of Oslo in the coming major races.

I left Oslo with too much confidence. I'd beaten the best in the world. I thought I was the woman to beat in the 400-meter hurdles. But my confidence was short-lived. As the US Nationals and World Championships rounded into view, I started to notice a problem with my training. I wasn't really improving when it came to my hurdling. I was actually getting worse.

DOWNTURN

The problems started as soon as I left Kentucky. There I'd learned a technical approach to hurdling from Coach Flo. While other coaches focused on endurance or speed, Coach Flo prioritized technique. How was I pushing off the blocks? Was I pushing into the hurdles without breaking my stride? Was I staying as low as I possibly could as I cleared them?

Once I left that training environment, the skills slowly began to dwindle. There had been such a specific way I had learned to be efficient that no longer training that way became apparent in my performance. I tried my best to replicate on my own the information I had learned, but it wasn't sticking. It was clear that I had a real shot at a World Championship, but as my year at Kentucky and all that technical training retreated further into my memory and away from my day-to-day habits on the track, I knew I was leaving more on the table. It was frustrating. I always prided myself on a continual progression. Each year, by the grace of God, I always seemed to get faster, but this felt like I was slowly beginning to roll the other direction. I began to second-guess everything.

Maybe it was the hurdling problem. Maybe it was my young age. Maybe it was the newness of my current situation. Or maybe it was that old fear, that tendency to run from my problems, that made me complacent. Whatever the reason, the reality was I brought it upon myself. I was so fixated on the highs of being a professional track athlete that I let the essence of the job slip away—performance. I missed too many training days that first year as a professional. I was the queen of excuses. If I didn't feel like training, I'd say my feet hurt, and I didn't want to aggravate my stress fracture. I'd say I wasn't feeling well. I'd say something came up. I think I missed as many as forty days of training in the lead-up to the US Nationals and World Championships. Way too much. Whatever the ultimate reason, the reality was, when I showed up in Des Moines for the US Nationals in July 2019, I thought I was ready for my first major race because I'd beaten Dalilah the month before. I was not.

Due to a small field of competitors, what normally would be three qualifying rounds was cut to two. I was relieved—one less race to run that weekend. But later, I was gutted when I found out Dalilah and I were both listed in the first heat. I had to race her twice now? Goodness gracious, I couldn't catch a break. Luckily, this was not the one that counted most, so all I had to do was qualify for the final. Which I did, coming in second, but just by a bit, to none other than Dalilah.

This meet was the first time I'd seen or heard from Dalilah since the race in Oslo. NBC Sports was covering the event. One commentator called me "maybe the biggest prodigy in the history of the sport."[4] If he only knew how undisciplined I'd been, how anxious I was about the hurdles. The media focused on the matchup between the two of us in the final, but that heat was, without a doubt, the best collection of talent I'd ever raced against. Shamier Little started in lane five, one behind me. She was a two-time defending champion, including the previous year. Dalilah was in lane four. Ashley Spencer was beside her in lane three. I hadn't raced against Ashley since she won the bronze medal at the 2016 Olympics. The NCAA champion, Anna Cockrell, was in lane two.

At race time, the rain had stopped, but the track was still wet. In those conditions, no one was anticipating what came next.

From the opening gunshot, Dalilah went on a tear. Even though she was in lane four, she had already nosed ahead of everyone by the time she reached the 80-meter mark. I gave it everything I had, running a strong race. My 52.88 time was one of the fastest I'd ever run, less than a half-second from Yuliya Pechonkina's sixteen-year-old record. But that day, Pechonkina's world record became a former record as Dalilah crossed the finish line in 52.20.

I was shocked. Stunned. Confused. Once I'd beaten Dalilah, I'd naively thought I knew what she had in the tank. Yet, she beat me. Not just beat me but demolished me—and took the record I had been dreaming of with her. Sheesh.

REMATCH IN DOHA

The World Championships were later that year. Doha, the capital of Qatar, was hosting them in October. I had two months to figure out how to beat Dalilah.

When I got home, the familiar anxiety returned, particularly during training when, one day, I mistimed my jump, slammed into a hurdle, and crashed into the track. It was embarrassing. Stupid. Completely avoidable. And I had no idea how to fix it. No sense of control.

Professional athletes don't love the unpredictable. I despised it. As summer turned into fall and the World Championships quickly approached, I found myself with less and less control over what was coming and less and less confidence I was progressing or getting better. There was not enough time left to fix my problems. It may have been my overthinking about the entire thing, but at some point, I stopped trying to fix my approach to the hurdles—it was too close to Doha to make a drastic change in my technique. Instead, my coach and I put the equivalent of a Band-Aid on the problem. We moved the starting blocks back two feet from where they were normally positioned by the starting line. Yes, this meant I would be starting the race at a deficit: two feet behind the other runners. But it would allow me to take twenty-three full steps before the first hurdle. For months, I'd been taking twenty-three steps but stumbling as I approached the first hurdle. That was why I bulldozed the first barrier in Oslo; I was too close. My coach and I couldn't figure out why, and we had run out of time. The two-foot deficit was our only solution.

I did manage to drastically improve my speed and conditioning between Des Moines and Doha. I was so shaken by the loss to Dalilah, so haunted by the defeat I hadn't seen coming, I trained at a ferocious pace over the next two months. I ran sprint after sprint—my coach's preferred training drill—until I thought I might vomit. But no matter how strong I was off the blocks, no matter how fast I could run on the straightaways, there were still those ten hurdles I had to jump over. And I still feared I wouldn't be able to clear them effectively.

I remember exactly how hot it was in Doha that year. How could I forget 120 degrees? The sweat that had no choice but to accumulate in all sorts of uncomfortable places? The gasps for air as the thick humidity took my breath away? Thank goodness the track where we'd be competing had a roof . . . and air-conditioning.

My training in Doha started a week before my first heat. I was so eager to get back on the track and get through the tension of this meet that the days seemed to stretch on forever. The anticipation of this race ate at me. Other than my training, I hardly did anything. I watched a lot of Netflix. I'd FaceTime friends back in the States, even though it was the middle of the night back home when it was the middle of the day in Doha. I prayed some, read a little, and waited, struggling with prerace anxiety I hadn't felt since the 2016 Olympics. My talks with God were brief. I wasn't sure he even heard me, or if I even believed what I was saying. It was mainly me asking him to let me win and break the record.

When race day finally arrived, there was an electricity in the air. It seemed that something special was going to happen. I couldn't help but wonder if it was my turn to break the world record. With an abundance of nervous energy, I went through my warm-up routine and settled in for the prerace announcements and introductions. I don't remember the camera zooming in on me. I was too focused on what was ahead.

I ran brilliantly that night. Under the Doha lights, in one of the most beautiful stadiums I've ever raced in, no one had ever been faster between the hurdles. But on the eighth hurdle, it was as if my body screeched to a halt. I slowed down, stuttered, and barely cleared the hurdle. That slight imperfection in my technique would prove to be the difference. By the time we'd cleared the last hurdle, I was trailing only Dalilah. The rest of the field was far behind. I gave it everything I had over that final stretch, finishing with a time of 52.23. It was the third fastest time in the history of the 400-meter hurdles. Three months earlier, it would have been the world record. But that night in Doha, Dalilah broke her own record by 0.04 seconds. Her time of 52.16 was the fastest ever, and less than a tenth of a second ahead of me.

As I collapsed onto the track, gasping for breath, I remember looking over and seeing a Team USA official cheering. For some reason, I thought he was cheering for both Dalilah and me. I assumed he was celebrating that the Americans had just taken first and second. He wasn't. His praise, rightfully, was only for the new world record holder. I didn't want to hear the congratulations. I didn't want to be told that I'd just run a brilliant race. I knew the truth. I'd fallen short, yet again. I've never been so disappointed, so completely crushed, after a race.

After putting on a smile, congratulating Dalilah for her extraordinary achievement, and taking pictures with the American flag, I found my dad in the tunnel. When I saw him, I couldn't hold back the tears anymore. Coming in second at the World Championships broke me. I sobbed uncontrollably. There was a part of me that knew I'd just run a fast race and finished second. That wasn't bad for someone as young as I was. But I knew it wasn't enough. I wanted more. Most of all, I knew things could have been different. My preparation hadn't been right. My hurdle technique was flawed. I was ashamed because I knew I could have won. And to me, there was nothing worse than losing when you could have done something about it. Still, I put the smile back on to face the blunt questions from media and gracefully accept defeat, for now.

In that tunnel of the Doha stadium, I reached the lowest emotional point of my racing career. But I hadn't yet reached rock bottom. Not for me as a person. That was waiting for me when I returned to the States. Just a few weeks after Doha, I went back east, to see an old boyfriend. By the end of that trip, I was broken. I knew, without a doubt, that I needed help. I had no sense of control anymore. Everything that had once seemed to be my peace quickly became my nightmare. I couldn't fix myself. I couldn't let go of my fear, anxiety, and need for approval on my own.

> I knew, without a doubt, that I needed help. I had no sense of control anymore.

Doha and the days after were some of the most difficult of my life. But to this day, I wouldn't go back and change a thing. They showed me just how helpless I was, and that sense of need is the best thing that ever happened to me. It showed me how fickle my foundation was. Everyone is looking for something to stand firm on. Mine was my desire for success and acceptance. But I would soon learn the true purpose of my life and give up the endless chase of fool's gold.

Chapter 6

In the fall of 2019, I pinned my happiness on two things: my performance on the track and the return of a boyfriend. When I came up short in Doha, I turned to a relationship, hoping a guy would fulfill me and take away the pain of losing at the World Championships.

The guy I'm talking about had been an old high school boyfriend. We started dating a few months before the 2016 Olympics, then broke up five months later. Even though I ended the relationship, I kept coming back to it because it was familiar and comfortable. When my confidence was at an all-time low after my first professional season, I thought this man might provide the peace I was looking for.

Ever since I was a teenager, I desperately wanted to be in a relationship. I thought about it all the time. Throughout middle school and high school, I would imagine what it would be like to build a life with boys I knew. If a guy was cute and personable, I would play through different scenarios in my head, wondering if at last I had found "the one." I'd do love calculators online based on our first names, then follow up with a verbal test of how Sydney sounded before their last name. Disney really screwed me up in that way. They made it all look so simple: you meet a boy, you fall in love, you get married, and you're basically a princess. Why wasn't that how it worked?

Since our high school breakup, my ex and I still communicated from time to time. When I was feeling especially down about myself, I knew he would pick up when I called. So after my failure in Doha, I took a flight to one of his college football games, hoping to reignite our relationship and get my mojo back. After getting some food after his team's win, we sat down to have a real conversation. I needed validation, to know I was still wanted, needed, accepted. So I asked him a question I had wondered since we broke up in 2016.

"Do you think there's any possibility of us ever getting back together?" I was sure the answer would be yes. Not long ago, he'd told his mom that after college, he was going to marry me.

"I don't think so," he replied.

My stomach dropped. *Did he just say no? Did I just lose twice? Am I not who I think I am?*

He had more to say, but I remember only the rejection. I felt empty. Worthless. Everything I'd looked to for purpose was slowly crumbling in front of me. As my heart broke, I thought, *The only way I'm going to heal from this is a miracle from God.*

I had been running from God for years, fearful that truly following him would strip me of my freedom. I didn't care anymore; I just needed relief from the agony. When I came back to reality, he was talking about how focused he was on his career. I couldn't stay and listen anymore. I needed to get out of there as quickly as possible.

As I ordered my car to leave, we said our goodbyes. Before walking out the door, he asked, "Do you still want to be friends?"

"No," I replied. "No, I don't. Best of luck with everything; I truly hope it all works out."

That was the last time I saw him. Though my heart ached, deep down inside, a small piece of me knew this was actually the best thing for me.

The flight back home was quiet. I was numb. I couldn't make sense of all the chaos that was running loose in my life. How was I not good enough? I believed I had everything I needed to be great. The Instagram followers, the money, the status. I had worked so hard to make sure I was someone worth wanting, yet there I was, alone and completely broken.

At the root of my need for that relationship was a deep-seated sense of insecurity. From a young age, I struggled to believe I was truly beautiful. Self-confidence didn't come naturally to me, and it wasn't something I was encouraged to cultivate. I also hadn't yet learned the healthy view of self, worth, and purpose that is found in Christ. For that reason, I was easily influenced by other people's affirmation or rejection of me. That's unhealthy for any person, but especially a teenage girl with Instagram.

On this social media platform, I saw hundreds of young women who looked nothing like me. Yet these were the women guys liked to look at. I figured these girls were the standard of what a woman was supposed to be. Was I not a real woman? Was I lacking properties of what made a true woman? Did God do me dirty in this area of life? Would anyone love me for who I was created to be? So many worries. So many wonders. I didn't have a clear answer at the time, so I did everything imaginable to fill in the gap.

I learned how to do my makeup, and I learned how to do it well. Days off quickly turned into Instagram photo shoots. Whole afternoons were dedicated to capturing content worthy of catching an eye. I would tell myself it was "for building my brand" and that the followers would help my marketability. That's not completely wrong, but that's not why I did it at all. It gave me a dopamine hit. The likes, comments, and notifications rushing in. I craved the attention even if it was just for the day. I was so empty and broken from the trials of life that I was willing to accept any sort of adoration, even from a stranger. It never lasted, though. Not every picture was a hit. Followers came and went. One minute you're the craze, and the next the online crowd couldn't care less that your dog died. (Not my dog, but I'm sure someone's.) I let my worth be dictated by an algorithm. Where is the security in that? To live life dependent solely on external circumstances of those around me is to be at the mercy of people just as lost as myself. I knew there had to be a better way to live life, and I wondered if the time had finally come to stop running from God.

> I knew there had to be a better way to live life, and I wondered if the time had finally come to stop running from God.

A NEW PATH

I'd given everything to being a winner on the track and being accepted and loved off of it. Now, in less than a month, I'd lost everything I'd looked to for validation. In my darkest moments of late 2019, I sensed that God could be the solution to my problems. I'd believed in him and knew that at some point in my life, I should submit to him. But where would I start? At that point, I couldn't have told you how to cultivate a relationship with God or how he could give my life a purpose far beyond racing or romantic relationships. All I knew was that I needed him, desperately.

Growing up, I'd probably heard hundreds, maybe thousands, of lessons about God. I knew that many of those Bible lessons described God's love, forgiveness, grace, and patience. I knew that if I wanted to be a Christian, what I had to do was trust in his Son, Jesus, and he would forgive me of my sins and allow me to enter heaven when I died. Yet most of that truth didn't mean much to me at the time. What did stick was the idea that God was a judge.

From early childhood to age twenty, I thought of God as an all-powerful being who punished me when I made mistakes. That was his primary identity in my mind. I was terrified the bad things that happened in my life were God punishing me for some mistake I'd made or sin I'd committed. I also assumed he didn't want me to enjoy myself. I had this idea that the really good people in this world give up their comforts to serve God. Much of this notion came from encounters I had over the years with proclaiming Christians. The stigma that I would become a Bible nerd with no sense of personality completely contradicted my urge for acceptance. I thought Christians had no fun. They read their Bibles and prayed constantly. They shunned nice clothes, delicious food, and vacations. I thought I'd have to give up everything I enjoyed, possibly even running, if I was going to serve God and please him.

Because I had such a harsh view of God, I tried to avoid him. In college, I hardly ever went to church (it didn't help that mandatory team treatment was always scheduled for Sunday mornings at 10 a.m.). I did start going back to church after I moved to Los Angeles in the fall of 2018, but that was mostly because I was living with my mom. We went to a church that was a lot like the one we'd always gone to back in New Jersey, but I didn't go there to learn more about God or to grow in my relationship with him. I liked the music, appreciated the people, and usually left there encouraged or inspired, but never feeling closer to God. Yet as 2019 came to a close and I thought about all the changes I wanted to make in the new year, my relationship with God was at the top of the list. I just had to figure out how to start.

If I was going to start pursuing a deeper understanding of faith in God, I was going to have to do it myself. A year after moving with me out west, my mom had returned to New Jersey to be with my dad. I had just gotten my first car and felt I had a good sense of the landscape to where I could manage taking care of myself. Thankfully, my brothers had also just made the move to Los Angeles. They were living a few blocks away, pursuing their own careers on the track and in the classroom. Still, no longer sharing an apartment with my mom meant I couldn't depend on her to get me out the door each Sunday for church.

I started going back to the church we had attended when we first moved to LA. The sermons were encouraging, but I wanted to learn more. I wasn't retaining anything. I would capture one or two good lines that I would write in my notes on my phone, but nothing penetrated the heart. There was no sustainable change, but just as I was ready to start diving deeper, the entire world shut down.

STUCK INSIDE

For the first three months of 2020, COVID-19 was not on my radar. I don't typically watch the news or pay attention to the headlines. I vaguely remember hearing about a virus, but I didn't worry about it. My strength coach at the time told me COVID was dangerous for old, unhealthy people, not a problem for an athlete like myself. I took his word for it and went on with my life, keeping myself busy with training for the upcoming Olympic Games. Then one day in the middle of March, I couldn't avoid COVID anymore. Los Angeles County issued a stay-at-home order. Nonessential work and activities were canceled. The track was closed. So was church. I had nowhere to go and nothing to do. The break was only supposed to last a couple of weeks. But two weeks turned into three, and three into four. Next thing I knew, we seemed farther from the end of the restrictions than we did when they announced the stay-at-home order.

The NBA canceled its season. Major League Baseball couldn't get theirs started. The biggest thing happening in sports was the *Last Dance* documentary about Michael Jordan and the Chicago Bulls. As the stay-at-home order dragged on in Los Angeles and around the world, it seemed unlikely the Olympics would still happen. But I tried to keep training like they were. Every day, Coach Joanna and I would meet on Zoom. She designed a few drills for inside my apartment, but there's only so much you can do, especially as a hurdler, away from the track. I was able to go for runs around the neighborhood with my brother Taylor, who lived a few blocks away. That helped both with the training and the loneliness, but as the stay-at-home order dragged on, I became less and less motivated and started to feel more and more lonely, especially when there was no way to commune with church members other than text messages. After trying so hard to reconnect with church and God, I found myself no closer to either than I'd been in 2019, when I was still reeling from the loss at Doha and the ex-boyfriend debacle after the football game.

With no clue where to turn or what to do about my anxiety, fear, and loneliness, I called a psychologist I found online. Our first appointment, a Zoom call, lasted forty-five minutes. I don't remember everything we went over. I know we talked about how much I struggled to move on from my past and be present in the now. How I struggled with prerace anxiety and couldn't move on from multiple heartbreaks. We discussed how low I felt because of the results of the past couple of years, feeling defeated in my attempts to turn things around. And I'm sure there were standard questions about my family, childhood, and career. At the end of the call, the psychologist's remedy for my anguish came in the most unexpected form: sleeping pills and antidepressants. I remember going to the pharmacy, picking up the pills, driving back to my apartment, and holding the two bottles in my hand. I could not believe this was what it had come to. This was her answer for me. We had spoken for less than an hour, and not once did she try to counsel me through the situations. No advice for outlook or perspective moving forward. Just a written prescription that I could pick up from CVS.

Of all the tough times and disappointments I'd experienced during the past five years, this was the lowest of the low points. *There has to be a better way to deal with my problems,* I thought. *Medicine can't be the only answer. I want to fix my problems, not mask them.*

Now hear me out for a minute: I do believe that counseling is important, and of course medicine and quality treatment are a gift from God. Having the ability to talk through and discuss the deepest parts of life is one of the best ways to truly create change in one's thinking. After all, Proverbs 11:14 states, "Where there is no guidance, a people falls, but in an abundance of counselors there is safety." I knew that, for me, at that time, medicine wasn't the proper means to resolve my life's issues.

My problem wasn't physical; it was spiritual. I was sure of it. Deep down, I knew with certainty that much of the pain and hurt I had endured was because of unresolved issues. I was searching for help with that. And I think that's what was so frustrating. I knew I needed to overhaul my life, change how I thought about my worth and my purpose, but everywhere I went for help I was getting only temporary solutions for my problems. Remedies for the symptoms of anxiety and sleepless nights, not the disease of self-focus and a misplaced identity. I wanted to hear God's answer to the problems I was facing. I mean, who better to get insight from than the Creator of everything, right?

Stuck in my apartment with my dog, Laylay (the cutest golden-doodle ever), I spent more and more time on social media. Fan interactions became a regular part of my days. I even hosted a show on Instagram called *Saturday Night Vibes.* I'd plan for it all week. I'd transform my living room into a makeshift studio. I'd come up with skits, answer questions, play funny games, and bring on special guests, including fans, for talent shows. There were even some beautiful displays of spoken word poetry from some of my followers. It was a lot of fun, until it wasn't. In the middle of the third or fourth show, a fan exposed himself to me. My little outlet of joy quickly became desolate. Immediately, I shut down the Instagram live feed and canceled *Saturday Night Vibes*. Not only was it disrespectful to me, but I felt personally responsible for the young kids who were watching and had to witness that. A bummer, for sure, and another source of joy to add to the growing list of losses.

After I stopped my show, I turned to things like Netflix and Hulu. Occupying my time that way helped my mind escape to scenarios other than the one I was presently in. Bingeing shows, eating snacks, and petting my dog became my new routine.

RETRAINING

Back in March, the Olympics was officially postponed for a year. I was honestly relieved. That was the best thing to happen to me since the stay-at-home order had upended life for everyone. Now I had more than a year to fix my hurdles problem. At the time, I still didn't know how I was going to do that. Since the World Championships in Doha the previous October, I wasn't processing Coach Joanna's instructions well. Most of her drills were sprints designed to build my speed and power. They'd been effective. At the start of 2020, I'd never felt more in shape or stronger physically. But I'm the kind of competitor who can't ignore a problem. I have a hard time focusing on the positives when there's a glaring weakness. My inability to figure out the hurdles frustrated me so much, I considered doing something I told myself I'd never do: go back to my college program. Coach Flo was now leading the University of Texas track program, but he still coached a stable of elite runners. I didn't really want to go back. It had taken such a toll on me the first time. But he'd gotten results. I'd never been more confident in my hurdling technique than when I was working with him.

I thought about it every day. After an especially frustrating hurdle practice, I'd think, *Should I just suck it up and see if Coach Flo will take me back?* I started to discuss the idea with my parents, my trainer, my track agent. It seemed like the only way I could fix the problem. By God's providence, it never came to that.

In early May, the stay-at-home order loosened enough for the track at UCLA to reopen. It was one of the few tracks open to the public at the time. All kinds of people were there, including celebrities. I remember seeing the baseball player Alex Rodriguez walk by during a drill. The track had a fun, energetic, chaotic atmosphere. Everyone was happy to be outside. Fresh air felt almost euphoric. I would have gladly let bees get close to me, maybe even sting me, just to let me know I was alive.

Before COVID, there were three professional running groups in the city. One trained at UCLA, the other at USC, and a third in West LA. Now all three gathered at UCLA, often sharing the track. That's when I met Joanna's former coach, a legend who'd guided her to Olympic gold at the 2004 Olympics. I already knew all about Bobby Kersee. He'd coached Allyson Felix. He'd also coached Florence Griffith Joyner, also known as Flo Jo. She'd won several gold medals and broke the world record in the 100-meter sprint at the 1988 Olympics. And most famously, Jackie Joyner-Kersee, one of the greatest female athletes of all time. Bobby was her coach before he became her husband. I don't think there was a more famous couple in track-and-field, and Bobby was without a doubt the sport's most famous and decorated coach.

After I had a particularly frustrating day on the hurdles, Joanna asked Bobby if he'd be willing to come over twice a week as a hurdles consultant. I'll never forget our first lesson. I was nervous and didn't know what to expect. I knew that Bobby was an intense coach, willing to let his opinion be known in order to draw the best out of you. As I lined up on the blocks, Bobby started describing what my first five steps should feel like: "Keep your head down. Drive out for the first five steps like you're pulling a sled. When you come up, keep your stride open moving into the hurdle."

His commands made sense. I knew how to translate his words into actions. The goal here was to fix my start to the first hurdle. I was currently taking twenty-three steps from the starting line to the first hurdle, which was 45 meters away. During the previous season, I had been struggling to get twenty-two steps to the first hurdle (something I had done with ease in college); as a result, we moved my blocks back, making me run farther than everyone else. My hope was that Bobby's instruction would help eradicate that extra step and get me back down to twenty-two steps.

In my first rep following Bobby's instruction, I made it over the hurdle with no problem. Twenty-two steps and all. I was amazed. This was something I had been struggling with for months, yet he just strolled over in his New York Yankees hat, shared a few words, and just like that, it was fixed.

In the following weeks, I would look forward to the two days a week that Bobby would join Joanna and me. I'd devour Bobby's technical instruction and immediately see results on the track. Still, there were other days out of the week when he wasn't around. The overwhelming thought of losing to Dalilah again ate at me. I wondered if all the work we were doing there was going to be enough. I was fed up with myself and started thinking, *I can't do this anymore. I need to figure out what to do.* I was bent over on the side of the track, trying to hide my tears, when Bobby broke away from the group he was training and approached me.

"What's wrong?" he asked.

"Nothing," I lamely said back.

"Obviously, that's not true," he said.

I'm not sure why, but I opened up to Bobby.

"For the first time in my track career," I said, "I feel like I'm going backward. I've always prided myself on progressing every year, but for some reason I really feel like I'm moving in the wrong direction."

Bobby responded to my moment of weakness in the oddest way. He turned around and walked away. After retrieving something from his backpack, he brought it over to me. It was a wheel with different emotions labeled on it. More common emotions were in the middle: angry, happy, sad, mad. The farther from the center of the wheel it went, the more specific the words got to describe the feeling. Bobby handed it to me.

"I have a hard time expressing my emotions too," Bobby said. "So I want you to have this. Hopefully it will help you figure out how to identify what you're feeling." Then Bobby returned to his stable of runners, leaving me holding this quirky emotions wheel. At first, I was embarrassed. Here I was bawling my eyes out to the most decorated coach I'd ever met, and he barely even knew me. Yet I was encouraged that, even with a lack of history, he felt compelled to come over and see what was going on and offer some help.

That night, I studied that wheel to see what it was I was truly feeling. I started with *angry*. What was I angry about? I was angry about my current situation, how I felt helpless in it. The next column branched out to more intricate words. From the eight listed, I most related to *frustrated*. I was frustrated that things were not going my way, and it didn't seem to be improving. Finally, we got to the heart of it when I reached the last column. The word was *resentful*. This word, though true in the moment, was not something I was proud of. My resentment was projected on those around me such as Joanna; my agent, Wes; my parents; and others, all because I was going through trials. Looking back with twenty-twenty hindsight, I'd made something that wasn't life-changing seem like it was the end of the world. This would not be something I'd get real perspective on until years later. But this encounter with Bobby had at least given me a start—and some hope that something could change. I could change, and my technique could change too.

As for this moment in time, I had come to a decision: I wanted Bobby to be my coach. I got his number from my agent, gave him a call, and asked if we could meet. He agreed to a meeting, and in Bobby fashion, it was at the most random of places: California Pizza Kitchen.

As we ate, I told him everything I was feeling. I spoke in detail about my struggles with the hurdles. I let him know about my prerace anxiety and how much the loss in Doha had crushed me. And I asked him if he'd be willing to coach me.

"Before we talk about that," he said, "I want to know what your goals are. What do you want out of this sport? What do you want to accomplish before you're done?"

"I want to win the Olympics," I said immediately. "I want to break the world record. I want to be a world champion. And I don't want to cry in the tunnel after a race. Never again."

"I've been there," he said. "I've had those tears in tunnels after races, and I told myself never again."

"I am willing to coach you to your goals," he continued. "There's just one thing: I'm going to need your full trust in my plan. You have to be all in."

"Understood," I said. "I'm all in."

The rest of the meal, Bobby told me his plan. As he described how we'd train and how we would achieve my goals, I felt hope begin to emerge in my heart. This felt right, and I was beyond excited to get to work.

BUMPY TRANSITION

Before I could officially switch to Bobby, I had to talk to Coach Joanna. I was terrified of the conversation. I'd never let anyone go before. I'd never had a real job or spent a day in corporate America. Everything outside the track had always been handled by my parents, the companies I represented, or my agents. I called Wes and told him how much I was dreading the conversation. I was now a twenty-year-old woman. Joanna was in her midforties: a wife and mom. She is also a genuinely loving and kind person. We had truly bonded over our year and a half together. I hated to disappoint her.

"If you want, I can have that conversation for you," my agent said. Petrified of the task, I let him.

After he broke the news to Joanna, I called her to thank her for coaching me. As soon as we started talking, I wished I'd been the one to have that conversation with her. I knew immediately that having the news delivered in such an impersonal way hurt her. It also stung that I was going to Bobby, her former coach, whom she'd introduced me to.

Joanna said she could tell that our coach/athlete relationship was no longer working and was coming to an end. She acknowledged we weren't solving my hurdles problem together. "But I thought you would go back to your old coach from Kentucky, not Bobby," she said.

Joanna had been like a second mother to me. Her care for me ran much deeper than just an eight-lane track. She wanted to see me happy and tried her best to bring that joy into every practice we had. Hurting her in any way was unthinkable to me, yet it seemed I'd done it. Severing this relationship ate at me mentally for months.

But the chaos didn't end there. I then made the mistake of letting my dad break the news to my older brother, Taylor, who was also working with Joanna. "Why did I find out from Dad and not you?" was the first thing he said to me after hearing the news. He understood why I was making the change, but the lack of direct communication made our familial relationship feel strictly business.

I'd messed up. In order to avoid difficult conversations, I'd damaged relationships with people I cared about. Of the many lessons I learned in 2020, that was one of the toughest. You can't run from hard conversations. You can't hide from reality, even if you're afraid. If you want to compete at the highest level, you've got to make hard choices, but you've got to handle them the right way. This means having integrity. It was my responsibility to be honest with people I cared about and be honest about where my head was at moving forward. This was a situation that should have been filled with a healthy dose of both grace and truth, which sometimes means sacrificing your own comfort to give people the respect they deserve. That's something I will always remember from that mess of a time. You live; you learn.

Still, after I officially switched to training with Bobby in July 2020, I felt like I could breathe more. It seemed like some of the weight had been lifted from my shoulders. Exactly one year separated me from the Olympics. With Bobby, I was sure I'd be ready to face the hurdles.

> You can't hide from reality, even if you're afraid.

While the middle of 2020 brought answers on the track, it brought few off it. I felt like Christian in *The Pilgrim's Progress*, always carrying a weight on my shoulders, willing to go any-where, talk to anyone, or do anything to get it off of me. I was eagerly listening to sermons, talking to women at my church, and reading my Bible more, but I still wasn't understanding where to go next in my spiritual life. And I'm not sure I ever would have if the man who would become my husband hadn't sent me a private message on Instagram in the summer of 2020.

Chapter 7

I admit, it was a little vain—all right, a lot—but it was how I vetted guys back then. From time to time, I'd browse my Instagram followers, looking for the blue check mark by their names. Blue checks verified identity and status. As a twenty-one-year-old woman, it's hard not to be excited when someone like that decides to follow you. One evening in August, a few weeks after my twenty-first birthday, I took one of those self-indulgent strolls through my followers, on the hunt for new ones with the blue check mark that always gave me a little thrill. That's when I saw his name: Andre Levrone Jr. I'd never heard of him. I clicked on his profile. A Christian. *Hmm, interesting.* Football player. *Very interesting.* Wide receiver at the University of Virginia. A couple of years in the NFL, playing for the Baltimore Ravens and Carolina Panthers. And handsome. *Very* handsome. I scrolled through his photos. They were surprising, in the best possible way.

I browsed his page for a while, trying to see what the hype was about. Photos from his football career caught my eye, but not for the reason you'd think. On a picture of Andre running with the ball during practice, a teammate suspended in midair behind him, the caption read: "My hope is not in the path, my hope is in Jesus' promise."[5] Another photo showed him at the Museum of the Bible in Washington, DC, standing next to a sign with a caption that read: "66 books written by over 40 authors, spanning 4000 years. The pillars of Hope, faith, LOVE, & obedience that are inside make life so much more fulfilling!"[6] Another post honored his parents' wedding anniversary. In the caption, Andre thanked them for honoring their vows to each other for nearly three decades.[7]

Who is this guy? I thought. In three posts, he'd pointed to his hope in Jesus, described the Bible, and honored his parents. His Instagram account wasn't all about him. I didn't know guys did that. It all seemed way too good to be true. With no signs of a girlfriend in sight, I checked in with a friend from high school who'd attended the University of Virginia at the same time as Andre.

"Okay, girl, just be real with me," I said in my Instagram message to my friend. "What's the flaw? What am I missing?"

My friend quickly vouched for Andre. "He's a good guy," she said. "Passionate about football, his family, and the Lord." And yes, he was in fact single.

The more I scrolled through his page—and I admit I scrolled through it more than once that August—the more I read captions that weren't about him. Jesus was everywhere. There was no way to separate his faith from the rest of his life. That was different. Not how I lived. Yes, I believed in God. I went to church. I was reading the Bible and seeking him, listening to sermons and praying. But there was still something missing. I never felt like I fully integrated all that spiritual activity into the rest of my life. I kept them in separate zones, cut off from each other.

If you want a good analogy of how I was living, watch the Disney Pixar movie *Inside Out*. It tells the story of a junior high girl with a goofy, fun-loving personality who is addicted to hockey. Her life is represented by a series of islands. There's Family Island, Goofball Island, Hockey Island, and Friendship Island. After moving to a new state and losing much of the life that gave her a sense of identity, the main character begins to struggle emotionally. One by one, her islands begin to crumble.

Like the main character of that movie, I'd separated my life into islands: Relationship Island. Track Island. Friendship Island. Faith Island. And not all of them were thriving. What I didn't have a category for, but what I started to get glimpses of in Andre's Instagram account, was a life where all the islands had the same foundation, or at least a bridge connecting them to the mainland of faith in God. I'd always treated faith as another zone of my life, disconnected from school, family, or track. To Andre, that kind of interconnected lifestyle seemed to be as natural as breathing. It seemed that no matter what he did, Jesus got the credit. Beneath each of the islands that made up his identity—athlete, brother, son, Bible scholar—was Jesus. Being a disciple of Jesus was a firm foundation that guided every area of Andre's life. While his fine looks and blue check mark may have been the first things to grab my attention, his spiritual strength and obvious integrity held it. So I followed him back, hoping to get his attention.

But nothing happened for weeks. No private message from Andre. No comments on my posts. Nothing. Well, that seemed pointless. Maybe he wasn't interested in me in that way. If he was, I assumed he would have reached out to me already. Other guys would send a private message the same day they followed me. Nearly all were lame. I can't count the number of times a guy challenged me to a race. "Let's race. If I win, you have to let me take you out to dinner." I refuse to believe that's the best these guys could come up with. To assume I wouldn't leave them in the dust in a footrace was just not rational. Maybe think that one through, guys? In all seriousness, none of the messages I received made me think, *This one is different.*

For two weeks, I didn't hear from Andre—nothing. So mentally I moved on.

One day, I posted a selfie with the caption "Attention," a reference to a song I'd been listening to. I wasn't trying to get Andre's attention. Or anyone else's, for that matter. I was just being a little creative. Later that day, I was at a photo shoot. I checked my phone, and there it was: a DM from Andre. "You have my attention. How can I get yours?"

I tried not to freak out. *Stay calm*, I told myself as the photo shoot continued. I was happy, but I was also shocked. I was sure I'd never hear from Andre. Now there he was, sliding into my DMs. And not asking me to deliberately lose a race so he could take me to dinner. Ethics.

I didn't want to respond in an overtly flirtatious way, so I sent the most honest answer that came to mind. What does get my attention? "Do you have any food?"

"No," he replied, "but I have a good recipe. I'll send it to you so you can whip it up; it's an old faithful!" I'd later find out that Andre's "old faithful" was a chicken dish he'd googled right after my response.

I was impressed by Andre's creativity. He'd made it clear he wanted to talk more without being creepy, then he hadn't missed a beat when I'd sent him an out-of-left-field response. Points for effort.

The conversation quickly moved from food to our shared passion: sports. At some point that evening, Andre told me he had an ankle injury. "Maybe you can help me with my rehab?" he asked jokingly. "You have any good exercises?"

I told him I did, then he asked for my phone number. That way we could talk more about those "exercises." I appreciated the not-so-subtle ways Andre went about flirting. He made it obvious he was interested but tried to keep it fun and lighthearted.

I wrote "Sydney's Strength System" on a piece of paper. "Price tag: one billion dollars. P.S. here's my phone number if you want to discuss." I took a photo of the paper and sent it to Andre. He messaged me about a "consultation," and after teasing that he would have his insurance foot the bill, the conversation permanently moved off social media.

At the time, Andre lived in Columbia, Maryland—thirty miles northeast of Washington, DC. After leaving the NFL six months before we met, he accepted a job offer from a reputable commercial real estate firm. He had spent the previous two years on and off three NFL teams (the Baltimore Ravens, Jacksonville Jaguars, and Carolina Panthers). It was certainly a time of adjustment for him.

After texting back and forth that evening, we set a FaceTime

date for the following afternoon. That Sunday afternoon, Andre
FaceTimed me from a park near his house. He was sitting by a
fountain reading a book. Points for being wholesome.

We talked about our childhoods. The similarities and differences between our families. We'd both grown up in church and
around sports. We realized we had both competed at the AAU
Junior Olympic Games in Knoxville, Tennessee, back in 2007.
We shared similar friends in high school and college, plus a love
for classic Disney movies. In many ways, we were very alike, but
our families were much different. Mine was quiet, more reserved,
not as quick to confront. Andre's was the opposite. They were
outspoken, type A personalities. Full of passion and zeal for what
they believed.

I quickly learned that all Andre's references to God and the
Bible on Instagram were not a show. His convictions motivated
every aspect of his life. No matter the subject, he could make a
connection to his faith. Near the end of our first conversation,
Andre told me about a Bible study group he was part of. It was
almost entirely athletes, NFL players, and men and women who
played Division I sports. "You're welcome to join," Andre said.
"I'd be happy to send you the link. No pressure."

As soon as we ended the call, I texted him and asked for that
link. I wanted to make sure he knew I was serious about growing
in my faith. Even if this went nowhere, and we ended up simply
being friends, Andre seemed like someone I could learn from. So
I joined the group. Though I thought Andre's Bible study might
be intimidating for someone with minimal theological insight like
me, I knew a deeper understanding of the gospel was worth the
discomfort.

Over the next five weeks, Andre and I talked nearly every

day. And we often talked about our faith. He once asked how Jesus made a difference in my life. I didn't have a great answer to that question. I told him that I'd started going back to church after the World Championships the previous year, but there was still so much I didn't understand about God or the Bible. So we started reading the Bible together when we'd talk. Andre would stop from time to time and explain what we were reading. I was afraid to say the wrong thing, so I let him do most of the talking while I just listened. It was refreshing, having a guy lead in such a strong way. I'd never dated a guy who was so passionate about something beyond me or himself. It was clear that Andre's first priority was not me; it was his relationship with Jesus Christ. That made him all the more attractive to me.

REAL INTENTIONS

Fast-forward one month. It was the first week of October. Andre and I were meeting in person for the first time. He explained that he was coming to Los Angeles for a meeting . . . during COVID. Sure. After his "meeting" (or lunch with a friend), we met for dinner in Santa Monica. At the time, I was still new to driving—I'd just learned the year before—and I was terrified of parking structures with tight parking spaces and tighter turns, so I decided to park four blocks away at my physical therapist's office: an area I knew well that had street parking. As I walked up to the restaurant, I saw Andre for the first time. The first thing I noticed was his height. At six-foot-three, he was much taller than I expected. The second was his outfit choice: a Jordan sweatsuit. I had on jeans, a cute top, and some New Balance sneakers. And the restaurant had an average ambience. I felt like asking him, "You do know we're on a date, right?" Later, Andre would tell me he'd intentionally chosen a casual meeting and an outfit I might see him wearing on an ordinary day. He wanted to be a genuine version of his everyday self.

When I reached him, he flashed a welcoming smile, extended his arm, and we executed the "church" side hug. As we sat down for dinner, our conversation just began to flow. I liked this guy. Andre had a great sense of humor and truly seemed interested in what I had to say. As the meal progressed, I kept thinking, *Where's the flaw? What am I missing? Why is "Mr. Perfect" still single? Something must be wrong with him.*

Less than a year earlier, my heart had been torn to pieces. I was terrified of that happening again. I couldn't see any red flags in Andre, but I couldn't help but wonder if they were there, lurking in the shadows. I hadn't yet been in a relationship with a man who lived a life devoted to honoring God. I didn't yet realize that was why I could trust Andre. Not because of who he was on his own but because of who God was making him to be.

After the meal, we walked over by the ocean and talked. As we stood there, listening to the waves crash against the shore, Andre took the conversation in a more serious direction. He told me about mistakes he'd made in his past relationships, how he'd eagerly started dating without truly knowing the other person. He said he didn't want to do that anymore. Now he intended to build a foundation on friendship and the love of Christ.

"I want to be completely honest with you," he said. Then he gave me an overview of where he was in his life and where he was looking to go. He shared past failings regarding his purity and desires. He put everything in the open, not hiding aspects of his life others would have concealed. At the time, he was twenty-five and I was twenty-one. I'd been accustomed to going to the movies for a date, telling lots of jokes and stories, not discussing real and pressing topics. I appreciated his honesty, but it made me uncomfortable. I had no idea how I was supposed to respond to it. We had only been getting to know each other for a little over a month.

After our conversation, Andre walked me back to my car. When we arrived, we hugged goodbye. As I went to open my door, he stepped in to open it for me. Stubbornly insisting on doing it myself, I told him I was "fine." I then proceeded to get in my car, say goodbye, and drive off. *Why didn't I just let him open the door?* I thought. He was trying to be a gentleman. I should have at least offered him a ride, but I was flustered by all the information he had shared, and all I could think about was being alone to process it. When I arrived home, I texted him and apologized for beating it out of there so fast.

That night, as I reflected on my evening with Andre, I found myself struggling with fear. I was afraid of how vulnerable he was and what that would mean for me. I wanted to tell him this, but I felt like I needed to convey my concerns in a way that was mature and biblical. I asked a counselor for advice. She pointed me to Proverbs 4:23: "Above all else, guard your heart, for everything you do flows from it" (NIV). This verse made sense based on hurt I had experienced in the past and my desire not to feel such emotional upheaval again. I thought it was good advice, so I wrote down a speech I would deliver to Andre the next day. I would tell him we were moving too fast and needed to take a step back.

That next day was cold and cloudy, but we met at the beach and brought some food to share. I wanted to show Andre what

I did daily—go to the beach and read. I began rattling off my memorized speech, including the "guard your heart" instruction from Proverbs.

Halfway through my prepared speech, Andre said, "Can I stop you?"

I paused, seeing sincerity and kindness on Andre's face. "I just want to say, I don't think that verse applies to this situation. Proverbs 4 depicts a father instructing his son to remain committed to the godly wisdom that has been instilled in him and not to veer onto the path of the wicked. So yes, we ought to guard our hearts—from the sin and selfishness that is so prevalent in this world—but don't you think we ought to embrace people and things that encourage us in godliness? I guess my question for you is, which category would you place me in?"

I was floored. Embarrassed. Also impressed. And I had no idea what to say next. I had come in prepared, eager to tell him what was on my mind, thinking I was doing what God wanted me to. Now I wasn't sure. Andre didn't let me feel foolish for long. He patiently explained again why he had been so honest. "I don't want to sugarcoat anything," he said. "I know what I'm looking for in a person one day. I'm not ashamed of my past because I know that Christ has saved me from it. Being able to share that and be up front with you is freeing for me."

Whew. No man had ever said anything like that to me before. I didn't understand how he'd gotten to a place where he could speak so openly about his past mistakes. For years, I'd tried to hide mine. Bury my shame. Run from it. Of course, that hadn't worked. Mistakes and insecurities haunted me nearly every day of my life. But now with Andre, my past didn't seem like something I needed to hide from. He was convinced that what mattered was right now. He had assurance that his past was not a hindrance to the man he was today because of the forgiveness of Jesus.

Who was I today? Where did I stand before God? What kind of relationship did I have with him at this moment? Those were the questions that mattered. Those were the questions I wanted to explore more, with Andre.

A DIFFERENT KIND OF GUY

I began to realize that Andre had been authentic because he didn't want me to be blindsided later when we started to get closer. I respected that. At twenty-one, I had never met a man like him. I had never had a conversation with a man about things that really mattered to each of us. I was treading new territory. A part of me was insecure. I wondered why Andre was pursuing me. He was handsome. He was articulate. He was successful, and he had a great family. *Why is he here?* I thought. I wondered what he saw in me.

The next morning, Andre texted me, reminding me that because of our date the night before, we had missed our weekly Bible study together. So before we began the day's activities, we planned to make up for it. On his way to my apartment, he stopped at Barnes and Noble. He bought me a study Bible with notes that would help me understand the meaning of each text. He told me, "I wanted to give you a Bible that's easy to read and understand. This one really helped me when I was first starting out." It was the sweetest gift I had ever received. Afterward, we drove thirty minutes south to have brunch with one of his football friends. The bond continued to grow.

At sunset, we returned to the beach. The weather was much nicer than the previous day. We set down a blanket and had a picnic dinner. Golden hues draped the sky as music played on our speaker. Andre had made a special playlist just for this moment. It was serene, watching the waves crash as the sun slowly set. This felt like the perfect moment. He asked if he could kiss me. I said the first thing that popped into my mind: "I just ate a sandwich, but yes, I guess so." We kissed, and you would have thought fireworks were going off.

That night, when I got back to my apartment after dropping off Andre at his hotel, I opened the Bible he had given me just to admire it. What I hadn't seen the first time, though, was a personalized message he left me on the inside cover. He said he was praying for me and was excited to see me blossom and experience "glorious growth." He included Scripture references and told me I was beautiful. No one had ever called me beautiful and talked about my spiritual growth at the same time. It made me feel truly seen. I felt like my worth was more than just being a good athlete or having an attractive face. He saw beauty in me, inside and out.

He was supposed to leave the following day, but neither of us wanted him to go. His three-day trip turned into four. We watched sermons, made brunch, and spent the whole day talking and laughing. Neither one of us wanted it to end, but Andre had to get back to Maryland for work. So he left the following day, and I would not see him for over a month and a half. Though the past four days had been the best of my life, I was afraid the distance would destroy the bond we'd built. The confidence I had while we were together left when he returned home.

This relationship can't be real, I thought. It was completely different from any relationship I'd been in before. And it seemed too good to be true. The old fears returned. I was terrified of getting hurt again. The last breakup had nearly destroyed me. I'd never been so lonely when it fully and completely ended a year earlier. Now here I was almost twelve months later, risking it all again, this time with a guy who seemed amazing. What if I opened up, committed to Andre, then I wasn't good enough for him? What if he broke up with me? Fear started running the show again, making me want to shut things down before they even started. The idea of things not working out overshadowed the possibility that this was God's plan for my life. Christian missionary and author Elisabeth Elliot once said, "Fear arises when we imagine that everything depends on us." I was under the impression that if things with Andre didn't work out, it would be because I had somehow failed. I was forgetting that if God has plans for you, no one, not even you, can stop them (1 Corinthians 2:9).

> If God has plans for you, no one, not even you, can stop them.

Several times before I saw Andre again, I tried to end the relationship before he could break my heart. I would send him texts like, "You don't want to be in a relationship with me. It's a mess over here."

Andre would hear none of it. "Do you like me?" he'd ask.

"Of course," I'd say.

"Well, I like you. So let's not live out of fear of what might happen."

It became evident: Andre wanted to be in this relationship. He had a desire to help me grow in whatever way he could. He was not going anywhere.

Six weeks after we met for the first time, Andre came back out to LA from Baltimore to see me. We grew in confidence of each other during that month and a half. We'd spent hours talking about not only ourselves and our relationship but also about the Bible. We'd continued to meet each week with the Bible study group he had invited me to after our first conversation. And with Andre's passion for Jesus, most of our one-on-one conversations turned to the Bible at some point. That meant so much to me. To have such meaningful conversations was refreshing to my soul. If there was a verse that came up in a text or conversation, we didn't talk about what that particular verse meant to us—what I'd always thought you did with the Bible. Instead, we discussed the author's intended meaning. I'd never thought about that before. *What did the people who wrote the Bible intend it to mean?* It was a great question. And though I'd read the Bible most of my life, I'd never thought about its original meaning. It was both foreign and thrilling to open it and talk about what it meant not just to me but what it was intended to convey to everyone, regardless of age, background, race, or gender.

I was more energized by my faith than ever. I wanted to do something to symbolize the newness of life I felt. During those six weeks between visits, I got baptized through the church I had been attending for the past couple of years in LA. I'd decided I was going to follow Jesus. I was willing to say that out loud. I could comprehend what my local church taught, but I still had not come to a place of repentance and surrender to Christ. Even though I had done what my church required for baptism—a series of studies through the Bible—I had not yet experienced the freedom that comes with genuine, saving faith.

Later that week, Andre came back out to Los Angeles. We

picked up like we never left. After a romantic dinner, we went back to watch a movie at my apartment. Before the film started, we exchanged greeting cards. We both knew where this was going. Andre asked me to read mine aloud first to him. He was beaming as he listened to my heartfelt words; I could tell they meant a lot to him. After, he read me his. It was the most beautiful composition ever arranged in my honor. The last line asked if I would be his girlfriend, and without hesitation, I said yes.

SPIRITUAL BREAKTHROUGH

In January 2021, just a few months into dating, I went to Arizona to train for a while. My training group and I spent a few weeks in Arizona because tracks in Los Angeles had closed again. While in Arizona, Andre came to visit me. During that visit, we experienced friction. We bickered and could not see eye to eye on several issues, such as our communication styles and my insecurity about his loyalty. He was pressing in to get to know the real Sydney, and that felt terrifying to me, especially since I thought he was a "super Christian," and I was still trying to get it.

"Maybe we should just call it," I said during a heated conversation. I immediately regretted giving in to my old fears, my tendency to run from conflict. "But I don't want to."

"Neither do I," Andre said.

We decided to take a break from our relationship to work on some things individually and see where God led. I especially needed to pay attention to growth in my spiritual life, and that was something I could not do while depending on Andre. That was a place in my heart only Jesus could fill.

On the last evening before we left Arizona, Andre and I decided to get together one last time. I'll admit, it was a strange decision. We'd just decided to take a break. Then, less than twenty-four hours later, we were hanging out again. The truth is, Andre and I were so comfortable around each other and so used to being together and talking about everything, I don't think we consciously thought about whether we should hang out that day. We just did.

When we got together, Andre suggested we listen to a sermon on Colossians 3. The message was on the topic of getting free from the old, sinful life. The words of Colossians 3:8–10 stood out to me:

> But now you must put them all away: anger, wrath, malice, slander, and obscene talk from your mouth. Do not lie to one another, seeing that you have put off the old self with its practices and have put on the new self, which is being renewed in knowledge in the image of its creator.

In that moment, it clicked. I realized that Christianity was still one of my "islands," like track, family, and relationships. It wasn't yet the foundation of every aspect of my life. I didn't yet see it as defining my life, only as part of it. I knew the Lord wanted every part of me. He wanted to take the pieces of my identity and renew them to bring him glory. He wanted my hopes and ambitions; he also wanted my insecurities and anxieties.

As I listened to the sermon, I finally understood that God could completely and permanently cleanse me from past wrongs and clothe me in his righteousness. It was the most beautiful realization of my life. Through Christ's death and his shed blood, I have been given forgiveness and mercy. This was not something I could earn or deserve. There were no works that would bring it about. Jesus saved me by grace through faith (Ephesians 2:8–9).

Not only did Jesus want my present, he also wanted my future. With him at the helm of my life, I could take my eyes off things of this world and my past infractions and look forward to a glorious future in his presence. A massive weight was lifted. I was never meant to lead my own life. I had tried that up to this point, and it landed me in the most unfortunate places. Surrendering to God was not giving up my freedom; it was finding it.

> Surrendering to God was not giving up my freedom; it was finding it.

After the sermon ended, I told Andre I believed God was asking me to repent of my sin and begin a new life in Christ. I wanted to set my mind on the things of God and put on the new self. Again, like Christian in *The Pilgrim's Progress*, I felt the weight slide off as I knelt before my Lord and Savior and prayed. I asked him to forgive me of my sin and how I'd tried to do things my own way. I asked him to do his will in my life, transform me to become more like Christ, and help me no longer live by the flesh but as a humble servant of my Savior, Jesus, empowered by the Holy Spirit.

An indescribable sense of joy and freedom came upon me in that moment. God had saved me. Andre and I stood and jumped around the room laughing and singing worship songs. I was free! Though I had been baptized two months earlier, I'd later come to understand that it wasn't baptism that saved me; it was faith in Jesus Christ (Romans 5:1). I had put the cart before the horse. What a person does doesn't change what they believe, but what they believe inevitably changes what they do. So it was with me. Upon understanding who Jesus was, what he did, and what he commanded, I recognized that the baptism was the public proclamation of my allegiance to him. Baptism declared that Jesus was Lord of my life, but faith in him saved me (1 Corinthians 1:17; Ephesians 2:5–8).[8]

I went home to California the next day feeling different. Even my voice and demeanor had changed. The difference was so evident that others noticed. That week, I had a photo shoot, and my regular hair and makeup stylists asked me about the change.

"You seem different," one of them said. "Lighter. Full of joy and peace." I laughed and told them it was Jesus. I was a new person. They were surprised but intrigued by my change. The whole room felt different.

Three days after Andre and I agreed to take a break from our relationship, he asked if we could have a two-minute phone call, just to share a few thoughts and encourage each other. Forty-five minutes later, we were no longer on a break.

> This was the best thing that has ever happened to me. Jesus had given me a new life.

Our conversation was even more fulfilling than before because it made sense. The lens through which I viewed life had shifted, and with that, so did our relationship. I can look back and know for sure this was the best thing that has ever happened to me. Jesus had given me a new life. What that looked like, I didn't yet know. But I knew everything had changed.

Chapter 8

It was supposed to be a routine checkup. For my dad, these kinds of doctor's visits were a normal part of life thanks to a heart condition he was born with: hypertrophic cardiomyopathy, also known as HCM. It keeps blood flow from reaching the heart and the rest of the body due to thickening of the heart's walls. Over the years, my dad acted like it was no big deal, just a small problem that required medicine and more doctors' appointments than he'd prefer. That's why my family didn't think much of it when he went to the hospital for treatment in January 2021. We all assumed he would be there for a few hours and then come home for dinner. But things didn't go as planned. His heart didn't respond well to the treatment. The doctors kept him overnight.

The next day, the doctor came back with unexpected news.

For reasons they couldn't fully explain, my dad's heart had responded negatively to the treatment. His heart was failing, and if he didn't get a transplant soon, it would give out.

At the time, Los Angeles tracks were shut down again because of COVID, so I was training in Arizona. When I had originally checked in with my parents, they seemed content, but once the doctor broke the news, it was obvious they were overwhelmed with disbelief.

A new heart? Right now? It didn't make sense. I remember my father calling me. I could tell in his voice things were off. He did his best to assure me that everything was going to be fine. He asked me to pray that he wouldn't have to wait longer than his heart could afford for the transplant. None of it made sense. As he talked, the only thing running through my mind was fear. His heart condition had always seemed so manageable. He'd never had any serious complications from it. He'd always been in good health, even up to a few weeks ago.

My dad wasn't the parent whose health was a cause of concern to me. Over the past five years, that had been my mom. Back in 2016, she'd had her own heart troubles. While taking me to get a prom dress, she started to feel a strange tingling sensation in her hands. She told me she felt off. Something wasn't right. We aborted the prom dress search and headed directly to the hospital. Somehow, she was able to drive us there safely. A few hours later, the doctors let us know that my mom had had a heart attack.

A what? I thought. Heart attacks were for older or unhealthy people, not a hardworking, track enthusiast mother of four. She wasn't a typical candidate for health problems, especially with her heart. Thankfully, she survived the heart attack with no long-term effects. But since then, I'd been concerned about her health much more than my dad's. I never would have imagined that if our family was facing another round of heart issues, it would be with him.

My dad was put on the waiting list for a heart transplant. No one, not even the doctors, had any clue how long he'd wait or if his damaged heart would keep pumping long enough for him to receive a new one. And if he did get a new heart, he had to withstand the operation. If that happened, his body would have to embrace its new organ, which was not guaranteed. A clean bill of health seemed suddenly remote. Almost impossible. It was all so uncertain. And as usual, I was struggling with the unknown.

While my mom and dad waited with seemingly infinite patience, I questioned God. Why was he allowing this to happen? I'd just given him every part of my life. Now his first act as the Lord of my life was going to be taking away my father? It didn't seem fair. Up to this point, the closest family member I'd lost had been my dad's younger brother, Uncle Russell. He was one of the biggest "Sydney" fans around. His joyful demeanor during a series of trials testified to how much he trusted in God's plan for his life. Just eight months earlier, my uncle had passed away from heart and lung failure.

His passing crushed me. For years, his encouragement on and off the track made me proud to perform and represent the McLaughlin name. I looked forward to hearing his feedback after meets and competitions. After I broke the collegiate record in the 400-meter hurdles, he predicted I would be "the best in the world." In the weeks before his passing, I prayed extra hard that God would spare his life, selfishly wanting him to watch me perform at the 2021 Olympic Games. But the Lord took him before Tokyo.

My uncle Russ's death hit close to home in part because he reminded me of my father. So when my dad called on that humid Arizona day to tell me about his failing heart, my emotions began swirling with worry that I was about to lose my father as well. It was the most terrifying feeling.

From time to time, I would wonder if my dad's sickness was my fault. Maybe I'd somehow displeased God, and this was my punishment. I knew that wasn't right. God wasn't the harsh, unloving judge I'd once assumed he was. Trials and suffering weren't necessarily a punishment. I'd been learning in the Bible that they were opportunities to grow, to learn patience and faith, to trust God and his plan. James 1:2–4 tells believers to "count it all joy" when we face trials of various kinds, for these trials are to test our faith. They produce steadfastness and teach us how to be like Christ. But I was still so new to being a Christian, I couldn't see how this could really be true about *this* trial. How could a just God allow my dad's heart to fail?

MORE UNCERTAINTY

On the track in early 2021, things were just as up in the air. There was no falling back on the familiar there. The year started with a brand-new race. For our first professional meet together, and my first race since the 2019 World Championships fifteen months earlier, Bobby entered me in a 60-meter hurdles in my home state of New Jersey. High school was the last time I ran the 60-meter hurdles. Bobby wanted me to compete in a race where my technique would be tested. Plus, he's the kind of coach who wants to see how you respond to uncomfortable circumstances. It gives him a good gauge of what kind of athlete he's working with.

Because I hadn't run this race competitively in over five years, it definitely qualified as uncomfortable. In the 60 meters, there is hardly any time between hurdles. Six or seven steps to the first (depending on how tall you are), then just three in between. If your reaction to the gun is slow, you'll get left behind. I don't know if I've ever felt more out of place than on that starting line. I had no idea what to expect. It didn't help that the current world record holder lined up next to me, and the rest of the field was stacked with some of the United States' best hurdlers. Not to mention I'd only practiced this distance for a week, so I couldn't begin to predict what was going to happen. I could finish first or last. Both seemed possible.

Between my dad's heart condition, my brand-new relationship with Andre, my new coach, and a race I hadn't run in years, the first couple of months of 2021 were filled with uncertainty. I'll admit, this wasn't how I'd thought 2021 would go, seeing as I had just surrendered my life to God. I don't think I ever said it out loud, but deep down I thought God would give me more answers. I didn't expect a voice to call out from the clouds, *Hey, Sydney, this is what's going to happen to your dad. This is how your race will go.* But I guess I thought I'd find some version of those answers each time I opened the Bible.

I'd always seen the Bible as a self-help book. Open it and get a boost of encouragement. Some practical tips for the day. A mantra for Mondays when you're irritable. That didn't happen in the winter of 2021. Instead, all the uncertainty, as well as my newfound hunger to understand the Bible, was slowly teaching me that I wasn't the center of the universe. God had a plan that was way bigger than my running, my relationships, and even my family's health. The Bible wasn't a road map to the best version of my life; it was a road map to God. And my job was to trust, obey, and be patient. Talk about a reality check. In a culture that teaches that we are to live our truths and do whatever makes us happy, God was completely tearing down those ideologies for me.

There are countless Bible passages that speak of how we are to become lowly and selfless, to become servants and even slaves of Christ (1 Corinthians 7:22). There are also lots of verses that say God is a kind, loving Father. As we serve him, he cares for us. As 1 John 3:1 says, "See what kind of love the Father has given to us, that we should be called children of God; and so we are." I also love how James 1:17 says it: "Every good gift and every perfect gift is from above, coming down from the Father of lights with whom there is no variation or shadow due to change."

God has everything under control. He promised that in Romans 8:28: "We know that God causes everything to work together for the good of those who love God and are called according to his purpose for them" (NLT). I knew I loved God. I knew he was in control of my life and my dad's life. And I knew he had a good purpose for me. I just didn't know what that purpose was yet. Thankfully, I wouldn't have to wait long until some answers came to light for my dad.

A week after my dad went on the waiting list, the doctors had life-saving news. He had a new heart. It was a miracle. Normally people wait months, even years, to receive the organ needed for a transplant. But God had provided one for my dad.

The day of the surgery was one of the most nerve-racking of my life. My family gathered via FaceTime to pray before he went in. I wondered if this was the last time I'd see him alive. After several hours of waiting, I got the phone call. His surgery was a success. The doctors told my mom the surgery went smoothly and, so far, his body was not rejecting its new engine. He was going to make a full recovery. *Thank you, God,* I thought.

TWO DIFFERENT PEOPLE

Filled with relief, I could now compete in the 60-meter hurdles with peace of mind.

I was feeling good physically too. My hurdling technique had improved significantly since the World Championships fifteen months earlier. I wasn't having as many problems during training. I'd even adjusted well to the shorter steps and different strategy of the 60-meter hurdles. The week before the race, I'd cleared the first hurdle in just seven steps, ideal for my height. Though this was a new skill, I was confident everything would be fine. *I got this,* I thought. *No problem.* Unfortunately, I did not have it.

The strategy was sound. The mindset was right. But when the gun sounded, I chucked the plan out the window as my competitive instinct, dormant for more than a year thanks to COVID, roared back to life.

The rest of the heat broke from the starting line at a furious pace. My instinct to stay with them tore through all the training and relearning I'd gone through in the past week. Instead of focusing on my rhythm, taking seven long strides to the first hurdle, I ran without patience, taking short jabs for strides, thinking it was the only way to keep up. It didn't work. I had chopped my steps trying to sprint with the other women, and now I was hurdling with the wrong leg. I flailed and stuttered my way to dead last in the field. Since I started running at six years old, I'd never finished last in a race. Not until my first competition after COVID, after I started dating Andre, after I switched coaches, after I became a Christian.

Almost as embarrassing as my performance was the postround interview on the track. NBC talked to me and the winner, Keni Harrison, at the same time. *Why am I here?* I thought. I felt like apologizing to her. She'd just soundly thumped me on the track, and her reward for winning was standing next to me and listening as I talked about trusting the process, learning how to jump from my nondominant leg, and being comfortable being uncomfortable.

Immediately after the loss, I returned to my hotel. Ready to be alone. Feeling sorry for myself. As I entered my room, I found balloons, flowers, and candy laid neatly on my bed. I suddenly remembered it was Valentine's Day.

I laid down in the dark, surrounded by Andre's gestures of affection, and started to cry. Moments later, there was a knock on the door. Andre entered with a bouquet of flowers. Still processing the embarrassment, I just wept. He consoled me with encouraging words I couldn't hear over the sound of my self-pity. I felt grateful for his kind, thoughtful, and very romantic gifts, but something in me wouldn't let me enjoy them. The negative thoughts outweighed the good, and for about an hour I cried.

That day, I wasn't sure how to be an attentive girlfriend and a professional athlete. Just a week earlier, I couldn't figure out how to focus on my dad's health and run in an important race for my career. And ever since I'd become a Christian, I'd struggled with being the meek and gentle kind of Christian I'd read about in the Bible and a competitor at the same time.

> In much of my life, I felt like I had to balance two different people.

In much of my life, I felt like I had to balance two different people. On the track, I had to care only about being successful, while in my relationship with Andre, I had to be willing to sacrifice for him. When competing, my objective was to leave others in my wake, but while I was with my family, I was called to put them before myself. And to succeed as a professional track athlete, I had to be aggressive, a killer competitor. Yet off the track, I wanted to be humble, gentle, and kind. The Bible talks about having a meek and gentle spirit, which 1 Peter 3:4 says is precious in the sight of God. That sounded great. Problem was, how do you do that one minute, then the next want nothing more than to be the best in the world and destroy everyone you compete against? When I became a Christian, I knew I wanted to stop living like a "double-minded man" (or woman, in this case), as James 1:8 describes. That kind of inconsistency between my thoughts and behavior did not honor God and, to be honest, was exhausting to live with.

Fortunately, I didn't have to figure all this out on my own. Now there were other believers in my life I could turn to. Between the NFL Bible study Andre had invited me to a few months earlier and another Bible study Andre started separately, there was plenty of counsel to hear from (Proverbs 15:22). Andre and I spent hours talking through my internal dilemma. Through those conversations, I began to realize that I didn't have to live with my version of a split personality: a kind, soft-spoken, humble-minded person off the track and a killer competitor on it. Both were consistent with the Christian life.

How? The reason starts with a fundamental truth about my newfound identity. As a Christian, I now existed to glorify God (1 Corinthians 6:19–20; Matthew 5:16). At the beginning of 2021, I was learning all the ways my life wasn't about me. It was about showing the world God's power, wisdom, kindness, love, and forgiveness. There were a bunch of different ways to do that. Off the track, I could do that by serving others, putting their needs before mine, and being excited when God did a remarkable work in their lives (Philippians 2:3–4). On the track, I glorified God by running with all my mind and body. I honored him when I gave every scrap of energy I had to the task at hand. Because this was the gift God gave me to use, and by using it to the best of my ability and humbly redirecting the attention to him, he would be glorified.

I began to resonate with the famous words from the movie *Chariots of Fire*, which tells the story of Eric Liddell, a Christian sprinter and missionary: "God made me fast. And when I run, I feel his pleasure."[9] That's an amazing thought. He takes pleasure in us doing what we were made for. And win, lose, or draw, to run the race well is to glorify him.

RUNNING WITHOUT FEAR

Thanks to COVID, 2021 was now an Olympic year. The US National Track and Field Championships, which would also serve as the qualifier for the Tokyo Games, were returning to Hayward Field on the campus of the University of Oregon in June. We were going back to Eugene. That was just four months away. I didn't just have spiritual issues to work through; I had to solve my hurdles problem—and fast.

After my last-place finish in New Jersey, my coach, Bobby, entered me in a 100-meter hurdles race, another shorter distance meant to challenge my hurdling technique. That didn't make any sense to a lot of people. I'd always been a 400-meter hurdles specialist. Neither I nor Bobby had given any hint I wasn't going to run in that event in the US Nationals and then at the Tokyo Olympics (assuming I made the team). So what was the point?

By insisting I run shorter races, Bobby was refusing to let me be comfortable. He knew the 100- or 60-meter hurdles forced me to confront my problem with the hurdles. Because the shorter distances had taller hurdles, I had to clean up my technique in order to clear them. There was no room for laziness. I couldn't rely on my foot speed to cover when I didn't execute correctly. Though my times started getting better as the season progressed—I hadn't finished dead last again after the debacle in New Jersey—I still wasn't comfortable. I dreaded each race. I was afraid to attack the hurdles like I knew I should. Finally, after months of dealing with my indecision on the track, Bobby had had enough of my fear.

I'd just run another lackluster heat, this time at a race in Los Angeles. I'd managed to qualify for the final just an hour later, but I had performed well below what I was capable of. As I stewed in my ongoing fear, Bobby pulled me aside in the warmup area and told me, in no uncertain terms, to cut it out.

"Attack the hurdles," he said, his voice as stern as it had ever been. "Stop overthinking it, and just go out there and get the job done."

Bobby didn't say anything magical. He didn't say anything

he hadn't said before (though I think he said it with more force than he ever had). From that moment on, I channeled his intensity as I prepared for the rest of the meet. Maybe this was the type of coaching I responded best to. Maybe his message finally got through. Maybe it was as simple as God giving me an extra dose of grace and peace that day. Whatever the reason, I had a breakthrough on the track.

What are you afraid of? I asked myself as I dug my feet into the blocks seconds before the race. *What's the worst that could happen? Why not just go out there and attack every hurdle? Why not run, for once, without fear?*

From the moment the gun went off until the finish line, I ran without fear. I don't know why I was able to push away the uncertainty and attack every hurdle, but it happened. I still didn't win the race, but it was the best time I'd run in my life in the event.

Something clicked that day. I realized that every time I stepped on the track, the only person holding me back was me. And I was determined not to let that happen anymore. Bobby must have seen the change—the belief I had after that meet—because from the point forward, he determined it was time to refocus on the 400-meter hurdles. He had seen all he needed to. We had just one race to go before US Nationals in Eugene—it was a smaller meet in Nashville. My execution wasn't perfect there, but my time was strong: 52.8 seconds. It was a world leading time, and the fastest season opener in history.

> I realized that every time I stepped on the track, the only person holding me back was me. And I was determined not to let that happen anymore.

From there, Bobby took me and Allyson Felix, who was preparing for her final shot at the Olympics, to the open tracks of Arizona for a tune-up before US Nationals. Arizona was the perfect place to escape the busyness of LA and focus on what we were planning to accomplish in Eugene. Allyson would get individual attention in the morning. I'd have it in the afternoon.

Bobby had a runner from a college in Florida pace me: he ran an open 400 while I did the hurdles. One afternoon, we were doing a time trial, and I took off strong. After the first hurdle, the rhythm felt right. *Fourteen to the next hurdle. Jump. Perfect landing. Fourteen to the next hurdle. Jump again.* The rhythm was the same through all the hurdles as I reached the finish cone he had marked out, gasping for breath, crouched over, out of oxygen, yet feeling strangely elated. Bobby walked over, a serious expression on his face.

"You just went fourteen steps between every hurdle," he announced. "I've never seen anyone do that."

By the end of our time in Arizona, I was clearing each hurdle in fourteen steps again and again. It's the best I'd ever felt on the track.

"You're going to win in Eugene," Bobby confidently declared. "And you're going to bring me a world record."

BACK TO EUGENE

When I arrived in Eugene, I couldn't help but go back five years, to the first time I tried to qualify for the Olympics, a sixteen-year-old girl with a serious case of impostor syndrome. So much had changed since the 2016 US Nationals. I didn't call my dad before my first race and tell him I didn't want to run. I wasn't terrified of the Olympics. I wasn't ignorant of my competition. Now I'd come to Eugene as one of the favorites not just to qualify but to win. There was even talk of a world record in the final. I was there with one of the greatest coaches in the sport, my family, and my boyfriend. Most importantly of all, I was there as a follower of Jesus. I was racing for his glory, not my own.

But some things were the exact same as 2016. First, Dalilah Muhammad. She was the woman to beat five years ago. She was still at the top of her game in 2021—the one runner who had consistently beat me over the last couple of years. And then there was the familiar anxiety. Despite my personal growth and my new faith, it still showed up in Eugene and tried to control that week.

A few days before my first heat, I was having a tough practice. The breakthrough I'd had in Arizona seemed to elude me. I was frustrated at myself. Anxious. And I let my emotions get the best of me. When Bobby saw me crying, he started lovingly yelling.

"Don't let the pressure get to you," he said. "Sydney, you are more prepared. You are faster. You are stronger than any of these girls. They can't hang with you. Simple as that. Just go out there and let your body do what it was made to do."

To keep it simple, I moved out of the house my family had rented for us in Eugene. It's not that I didn't want to be around them; I just needed to avoid the track talk. Hearing that some athletes had already competed and made the team built tension within me. My brother and mother understood why I changed locations. Taylor was scheduled to compete at the US Nationals too. A talented runner in his own right, he had a real shot at making the Olympic team. Then, just a few days before the trials began, he pulled his hamstring, reaggravating an injury he'd struggled with on and off for years. Few injuries are more frustrating for sprinters. Pulling a hamstring is like blowing a tire on the freeway. It makes it impossible to keep going. I felt terrible for my brother.

Now unable to train, Taylor still wanted to be close to the track, so he and my mom watched every event at the US Nationals, talking about the races, debating who would win. It was just too much track talk for me. I needed to keep it simple. Do whatever I could to get my mind off the track. So I checked into a hotel, wrote some Bible verses on some sticky notes, and placed them all over my room.

When it was finally time for the competition to begin after a week of waiting, a malfunction nearly derailed my first heat. Four times, a misfiring sensor told the officials there'd been a false start. A false start is when someone moves before the gun goes off. In the set position, when your backside is raised in the air, your whole body is tense. Sometimes an athlete can accidentally release that tension too soon before the race has begun, causing a false start and, often, disqualification. When that happens, you have to know how to refocus instantly. Get back on the blocks and get your body poised and ready to go again. You can't let your mind begin to wander. You have to get back on the line like nothing ever happened. But that day at the race, the false starts were actually false alarms. That was four opportunities to be distracted, to lose focus, to start the race the wrong way. Thankfully, I was prepared. Just a few days before, Bobby had put me through a bizarre day of training.

Each time I'd get on the blocks, he'd stop me with a series of seemingly pointless commands: "Stand up. Wait a minute. Go run a lap. Jog to the first turn, then come back."

What is he doing? I thought. *He sounds spastic.*

Bobby never explained his strategy. And I didn't understand the exercise until my first heat in Eugene. In any sprint event, you have to be ready for distractions, especially for false starts. Thanks to Bobby, I was able to stay focused and win my quarter-final heat. Then I cruised to victory in the second heat, setting up another showdown with Dalilah.

The day of the final dawned unusually warm for Eugene, Oregon. The weather had been an issue all week. The hotter-than-usual temperatures played havoc with the event, almost as much as the rain did two years earlier in Iowa. One runner even passed out on the track. Every athlete was having to hydrate more than ever just to stay limber. For me, the biggest issue was my knees. The track was so hot, it burned my knees every time I crouched into position. After exposing my knees to the track four times in the first heat and again in the second, I had a nasty cut forming. Add that to the list of distractions I had to deal with that week. I had to keep repeating: *Focus on God.*

The weather delayed the start of the 400-meter hurdles final until 9 p.m. It was an excruciatingly long time to wait. Bobby, my trainer Malachi, and I went through some warm-up exercises at a nearby track. Andre joined us, still trying to figure out how to best support me on race day. I admit I was not quite myself. When I'm locked in, filled with nervous energy, I don't always have a lot to say. This was just the third of my races Andre had seen, so we were still developing a rhythm on race day. Andre is naturally a fixer, and if he sees I'm frustrated or anxious, he wants to fix the problem, which I love about him. But the first few times he joined me on race day, he'd suggest an activity or start a conversation, thinking it would help with my prerace anxiety, and I had to let him know that the best thing he could do was just be there. Be present. Let me be in my own world. And be okay if I didn't say much. He respected that, and over time we developed a system that worked for us as competitors and as boyfriend and girlfriend.

When it was finally time to leave for the stadium, Bobby didn't join us. I'd heard this would happen. At major events, Bobby can't always watch his athletes compete in person. The nerves are too much for him. "I get a better view on TV anyway," Bobby said to me as Andre and I left for the stadium. Before departing, we all prayed. For the other two rounds, Andre had led the prayer, but for this one, I let the men know I'd take it. I prayed that God's will would be done, that he would be glorified, and that he would give me the strength to leave it all on the track. Unafraid, unashamed, all for God.

When we got there, I was shocked at the difference I felt. The woman who was warming up for those finals had almost nothing in common with the little girl who had no idea how to warm up five years earlier. The way I felt was unexplainable. Beyond prepared. Yes, the nervous energy was there, but I was channeling it into the event. Prayer and Scripture reading had marked the day. I'd read Psalm 31. I called my friend Christina. We prayed together. Talked a little about the race. Thanked God for the privilege of running. Gone was the terror, the fear of failure, the desire to be anywhere else but the track.

This was revolutionary for me.

As the warm-up ended and all eight of the finalists were called to the starting blocks, I was in my own world, not aware of anything

Unafraid, unashamed, all for God.

141

outside my lane. At that moment, I believed, truly believed, that God was going to carry me around the track. I was in his hands. For the first time at the starting line, I felt free to trust in God's plan. With my mind focused solely on him, there was no room for fear to creep in. He was my stronghold. I felt truly euphoric.

I was in lane six. Dalilah Muhammad was next to me, in lane seven. A half dozen more world-class athletes were on the field that night. The only one I was focused on was Dalilah. I knew she was going to push hard from the start. If I could stay with her through the first three-fourths of the race, I'd have a chance.

> For the first time at the starting line, I felt free to trust in God's plan.

The gun sounded, a clean start. As expected, Dalilah came roaring from the gate. She'd only run three times this season, three times since beating me in the World Championships nearly two years ago, but she was clearly in supreme shape.

Though the race was moving at a terrific pace, I could feel myself in rhythm. *Fourteen steps. Hurdle. Fourteen steps. Hurdle.* We reached the midway point. Dalilah was in the lead, obliterating everyone, except me. She was ahead but in sight. If I could stay with her for another couple of hurdles, I knew the race would be mine.

It's strange, knowing you're about to accomplish a lifelong dream, knowing that nothing can stop you. I had that feeling, that indescribable joy, when I reached the eighth hurdle. Dalilah was a single step ahead of me. And I felt content. Yes, my legs and lungs were burning. But there was a reservoir there. A massive kick I'd saved for the last 100 meters. As long as I cleared the last two hurdles, I knew first place was mine.

By the time we cleared the final hurdle, I was ahead. I pulled every ounce of energy I had for the final sprint to the finish line. As I approached it, everything went numb. I wasn't thinking about the pain; I was thinking about all the trials I had endured since my last major race. How long I had waited for this moment. This was it. I glanced to my left. As I crossed the finish line, I watched the clock stop at 51.90. *Oh. My. Goodness. I just broke the 52-second barrier for the first time in history.*

As soon as I crossed the finish line, I put my hands on my head and then crouched, overcome with emotion, my hand over my mouth. Dalilah walked over to me and put her hand out to congratulate me. I shook it, grateful to her for pushing me to it. It was encouraging to have good sportsmanship, especially between women. It meant a lot.

Still gasping for breath, and trying to process what just happened, I faced that now-familiar on-track interview.

"How did everything come together in such a perfect way tonight?"

"Trusting the process," I said. "There are a lot of things you can't see, but just having that childlike faith that everything is going to work out."

That night in Eugene, everything did work out. The world record felt like it was both a long time coming and that it happened suddenly. It was both a long rumble of thunder and a lightning strike. I'd been preparing for that moment my entire life. I believe God had planned it before time began. And then, all at once, I entered the record books. God carried me around the track for his glory, not my own. All it took was 51.90 seconds.

Chapter 9

A lot of world-class athletes—NBA stars, tennis champions, or Olympic medalists, for example—crave control. They take charge of everything from the equipment they use to every detail from their head down to their shoes. They have strong opinions about the way they are marketed and the message that's attached to them. They follow a strict routine, especially on game days: eating the same meals, wearing the same socks, taking the same length nap, warming up the same way and in the same place.

Why so much control? It limits interferences. Competing at the highest level requires all your focus and effort. That, I think, is what athletes love about competition, particularly in sports. It engrosses your mind and body. An athlete in top form is lost in the moment, forgetting everything except the task at hand. There's something exhilarating about that self-forgetfulness. The moment itself is a kind of natural high you can't get anywhere else. To chase that feeling, that flow state, athletes have to limit anything that can hinder them. It's harder to perform at the highest level and do what's required to win, if your heel has a blister because of poorly fitting shoes. If you're mentally drained from a PR crisis away from the track, your mind may be in two places at once. If you didn't sleep enough or eat a balanced meal leading up to game day, you might tire more quickly.

High-level athletes also want to control what they can because there's so much about their jobs they can't do anything about. If competing outside, they are subject to the whims of the weather. Most of the time the location of the event and the time of the competition are chosen for them. In a team sport, what they wear and their teammates are not up to them. And once the gun sounds or the whistle blows, they can't dictate what their competitors will or will not do. Especially when the stakes are so high, like when you're competing for a gold medal, all that lack of control can be the hardest reality. It can drive some athletes crazy, making them obsess about the smallest things they can control and become furious when someone disrupts their routine or interferes with their schedule.

There's only one way to deal with it. Control what you can control. Make the most of your training and preparation, then leave the rest to God.

I'd always tried my best to control what I could. I'd been fanatical about my preparation and eliminated as many unknowns and variables as I possibly could. But in the late summer of 2021, as the Olympics approached, it wasn't just the other athletes or the weather I couldn't control. It seemed like it was everything. And the reason for all that ambiguity? COVID-19. If I was going to win in Tokyo, I'd have to be okay with uncertainty. I'd have to embrace the unknown in ways I wasn't used to and had always resisted. I'd have to put my faith in a future I couldn't see and a process that was out of my hands.

Hebrews 11:1 says, "Now faith is the assurance of things hoped for, the conviction of things not seen." I had to choose faith in an invisible God, not leaning on my own understanding but having confidence that his perfect will was going to happen. Even when everything felt out of control.

At this point in the season, COVID was still controlling the world. Testing before meets, testing to get into restaurants, even testing to get into the gym was a normal part of life. So coming home after Eugene, I could only imagine how much that was going to be amplified once I got to Tokyo. But this wasn't the time for that, seeing how I had just accomplished my childhood dream of being a world record holder and winning a national title, as well as making my second Olympic team. I needed rest.

That's what I did for much of the first week back home after the trials. Bobby explained my need for rest in a way I never would have thought about. When you push your body to the limits, take it to a place no human body has ever gone before, it needs time to recover. Runners are like fine-tuned cars. When all the right parts are put in place and the engine is running fine, you take it out for a long drive. But you need to know when to put it back in the garage, because overuse can cause more damage than good, especially when you're pushing speeds no one has ever reached before. That's why I did nothing for that first week after Eugene. My nervous system, muscles, and brain all needed time to come back down from the adrenaline high of breaking the world record. That week was peaceful, but I knew the work was not done and that the real challenge was just getting started.

After my body was fully recovered, it was time to get back on the track. Unfortunately, I had nowhere to train. The track at UCLA, where I'd first joined Bobby a year earlier, was now rarely available for training. As surges of COVID-19 came and went throughout the season, Bobby and I had to look far and wide for a place to train. At times, I drove more than an hour from my apartment to the nearest available track. During particularly bad surges of the virus, it seemed that every track in Los Angeles was closed. When that happened, Bobby snuck me onto tracks. During one particularly frustrating day when we couldn't find anywhere to train, Bobby brought pliers and cut a hole in a fence so we could sneak onto a track. A few of these previous clandestine training sessions were shut down by police officers. It was insane. All we were trying to do was run around an oval, out in the open air, with nobody else around, yet it seemed almost illegal to try to get physical exercise. When looking for a track became too much of a hassle, Bobby took me out to the median—yes, a sliver of grass, dirt, and pavement—in the middle of San Vicente Boulevard, one of the busiest streets in Los Angeles. I know we looked absurd. An Olympic sprinter preparing for one of the biggest events of her life in the middle of a busy street.

COVID not only took away much of the control I had over my training, it also made it uncertain that I would get to compete

> I knew the work was not done and that the real challenge was just getting started.

in Tokyo at all. The Japanese government had all kinds of testing protocols and strict regulations for anyone entering the country, including the athletes. One positive test meant I couldn't travel, even if I didn't have any symptoms. A positive test at any point in Tokyo meant I wouldn't be allowed to compete, and I would be quarantined until I was eventually sent home. So as the Olympic Games drew closer and closer, I tried to see fewer and fewer people. I was either on the track, on the San Vicente median, or at home, trying to avoid people. That was it.

As the date of my trip to Tokyo came closer, the reality of my isolation grew. Unlike Rio, when my parents flew with me to Brazil and were alongside me for most of the Olympic experience, I wasn't going to have my mom and dad with me in Tokyo. The same was true of Andre and my siblings. None of my loved ones were allowed to make the trip. Even Bobby wasn't sure he was going to make it. Days before the trip, he still didn't have his passport. He'd sent it in to be updated months prior, but the government hadn't returned it to him yet. Without my family, I had no idea what to expect while I was in Tokyo. And with Bobby's trip to Tokyo in limbo, I had no idea what this experience would bring.

I had to constantly remind myself that even though my family, and possibly my coach, couldn't come with me, I wouldn't be alone in Tokyo. The same God who had carried me around the track in Eugene would be with me every step of the way. I'd qualified. It was clearly his plan for me to at least be on the team, to make the fourteen-hour plane ride and represent my country. I had to be okay with whatever happened next, even if it was the opposite of what I wanted. God's plan was sufficient, and I continued ingraining that in my mind even when the situation started to look grim.

QUARANTINE

Just a few days after landing in Tokyo, I received some terrifying news from a couple of USA coaches. One of my track-and-field teammates, a girl living in the same hall as me in the Olympic Village, had tested positive for COVID-19. We'd been in the same space, and even though we hadn't talked face-to-face, I was still considered a close contact and was going to have to quarantine for several days. Another Olympics, another quarantine—though the last time it had been self-imposed and only for a cold. Thankfully, I had my own room, but I still had to share hallways, common spaces, and bathrooms with other athletes. I wasn't sure if I had come into contact with anything she may have touched or been near, but the doctors assured me that chances were the germs had died off before then.

They told us that we had to quarantine and be tested twice as often to figure out whether we'd been infected. When one of my teammates asked if we could stay somewhere else so that we didn't get infected, they denied our request, claiming that we could only stay outside of the village if the entire US Track and Field team stayed outside the village. For example, gymnasts stayed in a hotel outside the Olympic Village because there were only five girls. The US Track and Field team included over one hundred athletes, so you can see why our request was denied. Still, the other women and I were frustrated by the situation.

Each day, we endured multiple rounds of testing, knowing that if we got a positive, our Olympic dreams were over. I became hyperaware of my body. *Am I showing any symptoms? Am I feeling tired, congested, or lightheaded?* Twice a day, I had to take a COVID-19 test. Those were always nerve-racking, facing the possibility that we had flown all the way to Tokyo just to not be able to compete.

The frustration of a familiar quarantine combined with the uncertainty surrounding the virus threatened to bring back my old anxieties, like a familiar but unwanted neighbor. My fears tried to take advantage of the fact that everything was out of my control. They wanted me to imagine the worst-case scenario. They asked me to dwell on what had already gone wrong, what could go wrong the rest of the Olympics, and the fact that I couldn't do anything about it. They wanted to use my lack of control to control me. It was a daily battle to keep that from happening—a battle that, in a way, I was grateful for.

The uncertainty and chaos forced me to rely on God instead of myself. Stuck in my room, I prayed for peace and joy. I reminded myself that God was in control. I thanked him for saving me from my sins. I thanked him for Andre and my friends who pointed me to Jesus. They would send me encouraging texts, recommending verses I should read and songs I should listen to. They prayed with me and prayed for me. Slowly, the fear waned.

God used a familiar foe to show me how far I'd come in five years. In Rio, fear drove me away from my problems. It sent me in search of any distraction that would help me forget about the anxiety I was feeling. In Tokyo, I didn't try to run from my fears. Instead, I worked to replace them with faith. One verse that I read while in Tokyo was Romans 8:6, which says, "The mind governed by the flesh is death, but the mind governed by the Spirit is life and peace" (NIV). I couldn't fix my mind on fleshly things; I had to fix my mind on the things of the Spirit. On heavenly things, like God's faithfulness, justice, and graciousness. He saw me in these moments when I needed him, when I was searching for him, and when I was leaning on him, and he provided all that I needed in the uncertainty. Yes, I was terrified of getting sick. I would have been crushed if I couldn't compete in Tokyo. But even as I faced that very real possibility, I had a place to go with my fears. I took them to God and trusted him for my future. As Corrie ten Boom said, "Never be afraid to trust an unknown future to a known God."[10] Now that I knew God, I knew he was holding me in his right hand (Isaiah 41:13, Psalm 73:23, Psalm 89:13, Exodus 15:6).

After the quarantine ended I was able to leave my room, though I still didn't escape the threat of COVID. There were reminders of its presence everywhere. I had to wear a mask wherever I went. Social distancing was a must. In the Olympic Village cafeteria, every table was divided into four sections, a plexiglass panel separating you from the others sitting at your table. Hand sanitizer was strategically placed at every entrance and exit, as well as seemingly every free space in between. Before I could start my day every morning, I had to register negative on a COVID test. The pandemic was a constant presence, and I had to work every day to make sure it didn't distract me from the reason I was there: to win a gold medal.

GETTING IN RHYTHM

When I finally got out on the track, I had five days until my first heat. Bobby still didn't have his passport, so I was on my own for training. Team USA had a training space an hour outside of Tokyo. I went there with Allyson a few times. She'd qualified in the 400-meters, so I followed her lead most days. A few times, our schedules didn't sync up, and I was at the track by myself, trying not to be distracted when I saw Dalilah working with her coach. *What are they working on?* I thought. Then the next thought was, *Don't worry about that. Focus on yourself.* Clearly, I needed Bobby.

Even though Bobby wasn't able to travel with me to Tokyo, I was hoping he could make it by my first heat. That didn't happen. "I'm getting my passport tomorrow," he told me the night before my first race. "I won't be there for your first heat, but you'll be fine." We then talked strategy. Bobby's confidence helped, but I still was unnerved by yet another unknown—going through race day without Coach.

Sleep didn't come easily that night. I called Andre, who was nearly a full day behind me. He calmed me down, reminded me that I'd done this race a thousand times before and that everything was going to be fine. We prayed together. Read a few Bible verses. I eventually went to sleep. But it seemed like only a few minutes after I nodded off, the alarm squawked. It was race day.

My first heat was scheduled for 9 a.m. I couldn't remember the last time I ran that early in the morning. I had to be out the door and ready to take the bus to the track by 6 a.m. When I got to the lobby, I saw a familiar face: Mike Holloway—or Mouse, as everyone called him—was waiting for me. He was the head coach of the US Track and Field team and also the longtime coach at the University of Florida. He was going to come with me to my first heat, watch me as I warmed up, and be there if I needed anything. His presence meant a lot and settled my nerves as I began my quest for gold.

I went through my warm-up routine. Mouse watched quietly. He seemed to sense that I'm not a talker on race day. The best thing he could do was just be there. I appreciated his presence so much. Sometimes you just need someone. They don't have to say anything special or do some magical preparation. Just knowing that they have your back means a lot.

At 9 a.m. Tokyo time, they called me and seven other women to the starting blocks. I'd waited five years for this moment. I had so little in common with the scared girl who had to run furiously to make it through the first heat back in Rio. Now I was a grown woman. A professional athlete. A favorite to win gold. And a Christian whose identity was not wrapped up in wins and losses. I was about to find out what all that meant on the track.

The gun sounded, and I didn't exactly launch myself onto the track. I daydreamed through the first 100 meters. I don't know if it was the time change or the empty stadium, but I was struggling to find the aggression I needed. Since I hadn't raced since the US Nationals, and I hadn't really pushed myself too much in practice, I wondered if all that rest had my legs feeling too relaxed. That didn't make the rest of the race easier. If anything, it made it harder because I had to exert more energy to pick up the pace instead of depending on the energy I already had to maintain it. Down the homestretch, I had to work a little harder than I liked to win the heat.

Though it wasn't a perfect race—my slow start and hurdle technique needed some tuning—I accomplished what I needed to. I was moving on to the semifinals and getting back into the aggressive, competitive mindset I was going to need the rest of the way.

Unlike the first heat, the second round would be at night. The 8 p.m. start time in two days meant I had nearly sixty hours to wait and prepare. I slept as late as I could the next day and relaxed in my room until the afternoon, trying to adjust my rhythm from a morning to a night race. When I finally made it out to the Team USA training center at 4 p.m., Bobby was at the track, setting up hurdles as if he'd been there the whole time.

"Hello, sir," I said, a wry smile on my face. "Where have you been?"

"Oh, so you missed me," he said. It was more statement than question.

"You know, just here at the Olympics. Nothing too important," I teased him.

Bobby's arrival was a jolt of confidence. It cleared away a big unknown. Now I could sense my shot at gold coming into view. I was ready for it. As we trained that afternoon under a gorgeous Japanese sunset, I started to feel more in control. Finally, all the pieces were in place. Nothing could stop me.

> Finally, all the pieces were in place. Nothing could stop me.

I was in the second of three heats the next day. Dalilah's was first. Moments before her race, it started raining. By the time they went around the track and it was my heat's turn, the rain was a torrent. It's a hurdler's worst nightmare. There is a higher chance you can easily slip, crash into the barriers, land in a puddle, or lose your balance. You can be the fastest, best-prepared runner, but in rain you can slip and your Olympic dream will come crashing down.

Bobby kept me focused on the goal. "You're going to get your rhythm through the first four hurdles," he said. "Then you're going to start your push at the midway point, and we're going to qualify with the fastest time."

The plan was all that was on my mind as I positioned my starting blocks. Just as I got them into place, an Olympic official approached me. "What do you think? You want to wait? See if the rain goes away?" At this point, it was absolutely pouring.

The question threw me off. *You're in charge,* I thought. *Why are you asking me? What about the other runners? Why ask me and not them?* I didn't know the point of the question, but I knew my answer.

"I want to go now," I said, wanting to get this heat over with, and also thinking the rain might get worse—which it did.

The gun sounded, and as I took off, I immediately realized that my vision was going to be a problem. I could hardly see. The rain stabbed my eyes, making the hurdles look like moving objects. I felt a bit like Michael Phelps in the 2008 Olympics when he swam a heat with water inside his goggles (though what he did during that heat was way more impressive; Phelps had to swim blind the entire way). Fortunately, I had years of training to fall back on. I got out of the gates without incident and managed to stay on my feet all the way around the track. I was in the finals with the fastest qualifying time.

I took a second to feel the weight of the moment as soon as I stepped out of the rain and left the Olympic Stadium. The next time I was there, I would be competing for gold.

GOING FOR GOLD

Twenty-four hours later, I went to bed, trying to get as much sleep as I could before the final. If I thought too much about the next day, I would start to feel anxious. My childhood dream of winning a gold medal depended on a lap I'd run at 11 a.m. the next day. The pressure and anticipation would be too much if I dwelled on them.

I called Andre. We prayed together. He distracted me with news from home. I told him I needed to go; I had to try to sleep. It didn't work. I was still tossing and turning. Then I remembered that my friend Christina sent me a link to an audio recording of calming Scripture readings meant to help you fall asleep. I don't remember which verses I listened to; I just remember feeling a sense of calm and peace. Eventually, I fell asleep for a few hours.

At 4 a.m. I was back up, and the preparation for the final race began. Hair and makeup. A light breakfast. With a couple of hours until the race, I left for the track. I felt strangely calm. I'm not the most mystical person, but I had a strong sense that God was with me. That he had planned this day long ago. I couldn't have felt more different than I did five years ago in Rio.

The strange, almost eerie sense of calm stayed with me until all eight runners were called to the starting blocks. I was in the fourth lane. One ahead of me, in lane five, was the Netherlands' Femke Bol. She was the reigning European champion and, by far, the biggest threat to Dalilah or myself. Dalilah was in lane seven, two lanes ahead of Femke. I knew, the other competitors knew, and everyone watching knew that Dalilah was going to set the pace. But no one expected her to set one so rapid.

The gun sounded and I took off, clearing the first couple of hurdles at the same moment as Femke in the lane next to me. I was running well. I remember thinking, *Is this real life? Am I really going for gold?* It didn't seem to compute. Then I looked ahead, and what I saw snapped me back to reality. In lane seven, Dalilah had opened a considerable lead. By the first turn, she was already passing the women in the lanes ahead of her. In a career built on strong starts, this was the fastest one Dalilah ever had.

Midway through the race, I realized how far behind I was. The instinct roared to life, and I started clearing hurdles with pure intentions of making up the gap. Still, as we reached the eighth hurdle, I was well behind. But I didn't panic. Desperate to speed up, I shortened my stride, stuttering a little bit into the ninth hurdle. I immediately thought, *This is just like Doha. Don't let this moment slip away; whatever leg comes next, just take it.*

I pushed into hurdle ten with my nondominant leg, clearing it as I had many times in practice. I was still a step behind Dalilah, but my momentum from the final hurdle had pushed me forward. I could sense that she was fading. And now there were no more hurdles. It was a sprint to the finish. I reached down, deeper than I'd ever reached before, and pulled out every reserve to make it to the finish line. A few steps away, I leaned forward—head down, chest out—and crossed the finish line 0.12 tenths of a second ahead of Dalilah.

I glanced to my left. *Is that what I think it is?* Another world record: 51.46. It really was a furious pace. Dalilah's 51.58 time was faster than my previous world record. I crouched down, exhausted and in awe of the moment. *I just won a gold medal,* I thought. And because I'd figured out those last two hurdles, I'd somehow beaten Dalilah again. For so long, she had been the standard in the 400-meter hurdles, one of the all-time greats. Winning an Olympic gold was sweet, and I knew she had pushed me to it.

As I stumbled off the track, still struggling to catch my

breath, all I wanted was to see my parents. Hug Andre. Watch him scream and jump with a smile that filled his whole face. But they weren't there. In fact, hardly anyone was in the stadium. Not even Bobby. Just like in Eugene, he was watching from the warm-up track. The only familiar face I saw was an old friend from high school named Sean who worked for NBC. He was holding a sign, cheering as I captured gold. As much as I cherish that day, I will always wish my loved ones could have been with me in person.

After the media interview and awards ceremony—where Dalilah, Femke, and I all wore masks that made us look like Bane from *Batman*—I called my parents.

"You made that one close, huh?" they said. I could almost hear the smiles on their faces.

"You're an Olympic champion!" Andre screamed when I FaceTimed him. "I'm so proud of you."

The next day, I found out that I would be competing in one of the final events of the Olympic Games as part of the US's 400-meter relay team. I'd be running alongside Dalilah, my teammate Allyson Felix, and my future teammate Athing Mu, who had just won the 800-meter gold. I was thrilled to be on the team but a little less thrilled when I found out that I would be the leadoff leg. I'd never run first in a 4-by-4 in my life. It's considered the longest leg and, in my opinion, the least fun to run. Still, I was grateful for the opportunity.

I ran well and had the lead when I handed the baton to Allyson. What a legendary moment that was. The first and only time I ever got to be in a race with her. What a full-circle moment. The four of us won gold. And we won it on the day I turned twenty-two. I couldn't think of a better birthday present.

FREEDOM TO FLY

The next day was the closing ceremonies. While the rest of the athletes in the village were preparing to walk through the stadium, I had other plans. When I got on the elevator with a crowd of Team USA members, I was the only one not wearing my uniform: the red, white, and blue Ralph Lauren tracksuit.

"Where are you going?" someone asked.

"You're not going to the closing ceremonies?" another said, a shocked tone in her voice.

"Not this time; I have other plans," I replied.

As the other athletes boarded the Team USA bus, I hopped in a taxi. It took me to downtown Tokyo. The first thing I needed was a meal, so in true Olympic fashion, I found a McDonald's. After enjoying my chicken nuggets and fries, it was time for dessert. Right across the alleyway was a café, and I ordered an incredible waffle with ice cream. It was the perfect splurge-day after my Olympics officially ended. From there, I got some coffee, then stopped by Tokyo's New Balance store. I had one more stop before I headed back to the Olympic Village. It was a familiar place.

Two years earlier, I had visited Tokyo to record a game show. While there, I'd decided, on a whim, to find a tattoo parlor and get a tiny cross tattooed on the inside of my ring finger. My only tattoo at that point. Thankfully, they were open two years later. I was worried the pandemic would have shut them down.

"You here for the Olympics?" the artists asked as I sat down. I said yes.

"How did you do?"

"Pretty well."

"Did you win a medal?"

Instead of answering the question, I pulled a gold medal out of my pocket and showed it to him.

"Oh wow! Look at that! What would you like? I'll do it for free," the artist said when he was finished admiring it.

I smiled as I answered, thinking about all those times I had stepped onto the track, feeling like I could run forever, that no one could stop me, that I was free from everything that held me back. I thought about the fears that had nearly derailed my life and career, that ruined my first Olympics, and that Christ set me free from the previous year. I thought about the freedom of my future. No condemnation. No punishment. Forever free thanks to Jesus' sacrifice. I thought of my dad's words moments before my first race when I was six years old: "Syd, be the butterfly."

Freedom from fear. Freedom to fly.

Freedom from fear. Freedom to fly. I told the artist, "A butterfly."

Chapter 10

Scottsdale, Arizona. It was the setting for a delayed birthday party, courtesy of the Tokyo Olympics. Of course, I wasn't going to complain about it. It was August 20, 2021, a couple of weeks since I returned home, two gold medals and a fresh tattoo in tow. My first week back, I vacationed with family in Palm Springs, probably my favorite place on earth. In Scottsdale, I was with friends, girls from the Bible study Andre invited me to when we started dating. Though I'd known these girls for only a year, they had become some of my closest friends. This was supposed to be a girls' weekend to celebrate my new year of life, as well as the hardware I'd just brought home. Yet I couldn't help but wonder if another celebration was on the horizon.

I started noticing how strangely everyone around me was acting as we prepared for dinner. My friends gave each other knowing looks, smiled, and giggled every time they glanced at me. Weirded out, I slipped into my room and touched up my makeup. I checked my dress. Made sure everything was in place. Why was I suddenly nervous? I wondered where Andre was at that moment. *Is he close by?* I thought. Earlier in the day, he had sent me pictures from back in Maryland, so why did I think he might be around? I told myself not to get ahead of myself. I didn't want to be disappointed if everyone was just being extra friendly tonight. After one last look in the mirror, I headed back out to the living room, where a videographer was waiting.

"We know you have a YouTube channel and thought it would be cool to get some content," one of my friends said, seeing my suspicion. Really? Content for the girl who only has like three videos? Yeah, Andre was definitely proposing.

We made our way from our Airbnb to the Four Seasons Resort, where we had a dinner reservation. I was driving, two of my friends were in the back seat, and the videographer sat in the passenger seat so he could videotape me. It was almost unbelievable. Surreal. I thought, *I am literally driving to my proposal*. I was sweating the entire drive.

The staff at the Four Seasons clearly knew what I suspected. They smiled when they saw me and the videographer capturing my every move. A waiter handed me an envelope and said since this was my birthday party (never mind my birthday was almost two weeks ago), my friends had made sure the patio was decorated in my honor. My heart started to pound. Shaking in my heels, I tried to hold myself together. I was excited. Nervous. This was it. I knew that Andre was waiting for me outside. Opening the envelope, I read a card handwritten by him, apologizing for his absence that evening. He let me know that he had left a present for me out on the lawn and hoped it would make up for his not being there. *Oh boy, here we go.*

When I saw him, I tried to keep my composure. I made sure to grip the railing as I headed down the stairs. *He may not want to go through with it if I faceplant right now,* I thought.

Before Andre got down on one knee, he did what he does so well: gave a glorious speech. He recalled the highs and lows of our relationship. He told me how much he loved me; he said he knew, more than he'd known almost anything else in his life, that God had brought the two of us together. Then he asked me to marry him.

It was the easiest decision of my life. I explained why in my Instagram post the next day:

Till this day I can't comprehend how someone who possesses everything I've prayed for has finally come into my life. Our growth together exceeds what the dates on a calendar show. I fall in love with you more and more each day off of the strength of your faith. Andre, you are the most God-fearing, passionate, honest, loving, hardworking, protective, and genuine man I've ever met. I see Jesus in you. And as a result it makes you so easy to love. I truly did not know the definition of love until I met you; a sacrificial choice to lay down your life for the wellbeing of another. With that being said, there is no one I'd rather lay down my life for. The calling God has on our lives goes far beyond our love for one another. This union will impact lives for his kingdom, and that's what excites me most. I have no fear. I will keep my eyes on you, as you keep your eyes on Him. You're the perfect man to lead me, and I cannot wait to follow.

Love,
Your future wife[11]

Later that night, lying in bed, staring at my new ring, I felt all the emotions. Joy. Excitement. A little bit of shock. It was surreal, having the man of my dreams put such a beautiful ring on my finger. But in the midst of the happiness, I could feel the anxiety working to be the moment's defining feature. I couldn't help but think of the perceptions of others on my getting engaged to Andre after only nine months. The worry tried to invent future crises so I would dwell on those. By this point, its playbook was familiar: make my life all about what I can't control and what's less than perfect.

The old me would have followed fear's playbook. She would have been so consumed by the potential problems with engagement, I doubt she would have lasted a week as a fiancée. But by God's grace, I was a new person. Christ had changed me, infused me with confidence in him and his plan, to know that he works all things together for the good of those who love him (Romans 8:28). I knew, without a doubt, he'd brought Andre and me together. I knew we wanted our relationship to be about him, not us. And I knew if I was going to honor him as I moved from girlfriend to wife,

> I was going to have to let go of my anxiety and trust God even when the future was unknown.

I was going to have to let go of my anxiety and trust God even when the future was unknown and Andre's and my relationship wasn't perfect. That truth led me into sleep that night in Arizona. I'd cling to it again and again in the coming months as Andre and I went through all kinds of unexpected challenges.

WEDDING PLANS

When I returned to Los Angeles with an engagement ring, it seemed like every day brought another grown-up decision. We had to decide when and where we were going to marry. Whatever day we got married couldn't interfere with my running season. But we also wanted to tie the knot outside on the East Coast to make sure family could be there. For that, spring—the middle of my season—was ideal. Whatever day we picked, we wanted to make sure Andre's best friend, who was his best man, could be there. He played in the NFL, so that took August through January out of the question. One decision. So many factors. And so many people affected, in big ways and small, by the date and location we would choose.

I think that's what I mean by grown-up decisions—when what you decide affects other people's lives. To me, that's the definition of adulting: being responsible for more than myself and my money, time, and schedule. Eventually, we decided on the first week of May. And we picked a venue in Virginia, not far from Charlottesville, where Andre went to college.

Once we'd picked a date and location for our wedding, we needed to let everyone know. My first conversation was with Bobby. He laughed when I told him the date.

"If you want to get married in the middle of the season, okay. I don't think I know any runners who have ever done that before," he said.

"I know," I said. "But this is the time that works for us. And I will make sure I am focused on track when on the track."

"All right," he said, a wry smile on his face. "If that's what you want to do, then that's what we're going to do. People will think you're crazy, but if you're willing to get the work done, we'll go for it."

In other words, *I'm going to push you that much harder since we've got to work around the wedding.* I wasn't just willing to work a little harder; I was glad for it. It made life simple. Go to the track each morning, push your body to its limits, then go home, take a shower, sit on the couch the rest of the day, and plan your wedding.

After I spoke to Bobby, we talked to our families. Not as easy.

Putting ourselves in our parents' place, it's easy to understand their concerns. Snagging a boyfriend who slid into my Instagram DMs probably didn't come across as the most reassuring life decision. And as I've said, Andre and I didn't get a lot of opportunities to spend time with family, to let them see our chemistry, our commitment to each other, and our common love for God. As much as we wish we'd grown up in the same town, attended the same school, and were high school sweethearts, that just wasn't our reality.

"Why not wait?" Parents, siblings, extended family, and friends asked us that question. "Why not let the people who care about you get to know you two as a couple?" We explained that while the nine months Andre and I dated may not have seemed like a long time, every part of it was intentional. Our relationship was centered on Christ, focused on honoring him, and fueled by endless love for each other. We were sure, even if others weren't. We also didn't want a long engagement. Less than a year was ideal. But I also wanted enough time to plan the biggest day of our lives. That's why we settled on May 2022. When we picked that date, we were confident that those we loved would be on board by the wedding. A few months from our big day, we realized that wasn't a guarantee. Everything was so brand-new, and since our families hadn't spent much time around each other, they still had a lot of questions about the family their child was marrying into.

I think it was especially hard for my parents at first. Since I was their youngest daughter, just twenty-two years old, marrying a guy she met on the internet, their parental concern was understandable. Andre and I had to work extra hard to show them how committed we were to each other and let them see the love we shared. After some difficult conversations and much prayer, everyone was on the same page. It brought clarity and joy to the situation. God gave us the wisdom to lovingly express our joint decisions when it came to the date, bridal party, cost, and location.

Looking back at the dynamic now, I am grateful that those difficult conversations took place. It put Andre and me in the driver's seat of our marriage and was a public declaration to those around us that we were serious about this union. We were going to have a wedding!

LIFE TOGETHER

While Andre and I were trying to navigate relationships with family, we also had to decide where to live. This decision introduced new kinds of uncertainty, frustrations, a few disagreements with Andre, and temptations to fear. At the time, Andre was working in commercial real estate in Baltimore. I was training with Bobby in Los Angeles. I didn't want to force Andre to quit his job and move across the country to support my career. He has always been very purpose driven—working toward a goal in mind, whether football or real estate. God had called him to work. It felt selfish to ask him to adjust his life completely to mine while I made no adjustments for him. Of course, we'd had conversations when we were dating about where we'd live and what Andre would do for work. We'd even talked about my career. How long would I run? Would I be willing to give it up if it was clear God had another plan for Andre and me? Before engagement, those had been interesting talking points, ways to get to know each other and fill the long hours of FaceTime and phone calls. Now they weren't theoretical. We actually had to decide: Your coast or mine? Your career or mine?

A month or so after Andre and I were engaged, it seemed like we found an ideal place to live: the same place we got engaged. A friend of Andre's offered him a job in Arizona as a personal trainer. It was an ideal job for Andre. He knows as much about physical fitness as anyone I've ever met, and he has a knack for encouraging and motivating people. He'd quickly become a valuable resource for my own fitness on and off the track. Not to mention all the knowledge he'd accumulated through years of playing football. Injuries were his best teacher. It seemed like a good fit for him and us. I could continue my career in a place I liked to train. Andre could start a new career. It would be a fresh start for both of us. There was just one problem: What about Bobby?

I couldn't ask Bobby to leave Los Angeles. I wasn't the only runner he coached. Not to mention he had called Los Angeles home for decades. But there would be no switching coaches. Bobby and I had developed too much of a bond.

For a few weeks, Bobby was open to the possibility of coaching me from LA. He'd fly out to Arizona a few times a month and FaceTime during practices to give me instructions and check on my progress. But after giving it some thought, Bobby decided that wasn't what was best for my career.

"I can't do long-distance coaching," Bobby said. He's as old-school as it gets, in the best possible way. "If I'm going to get your best from you, I got to be with you day in and day out."

I knew he was right. And I knew I couldn't leave Bobby.

With Arizona off the table, Andre didn't hesitate to quit his job and move to Los Angeles. Finally, after more than a year of getting to know each other from opposite coasts, we lived in the same city. No more figuring out time-zone differences. No more five-hour plane flights and a few short days together. No more FaceTime conversations after training. Now we could talk in person, every day. We could go to church as a couple, run errands with each other, and plan our wedding together. It was such a relief. It felt normal, the way life is supposed to be. There was just one problem: Andre didn't have a place to live until we got married.

As you read that last sentence, maybe you have questions: "Why was that a problem? Why not just have Andre move in with you? Why wouldn't you want to live together before you got married?"

Maybe you think everyone should live together for a while before getting married. After all, how can you really know if you want to spend the rest of your life with someone if you don't live with them first?

Those questions are common in today's culture. A lot of people would agree with you. It doesn't sound like a big deal. In fact, for a few weeks after Andre moved to Los Angeles, it wasn't to us either. Now, before we go any further, let me clarify. When I say "live together," I'm speaking of cohabitation. Living under the same roof. That's it. It was early 2022. We were getting married in May. It seemed like such a waste to pay for a hotel or find a short-term lease for an apartment when I had a second bedroom that no one had used since my mom moved back to New Jersey in 2019. So when Andre landed in LA, he slept for a few weeks in my spare bedroom.

"Why separate bedrooms? Why didn't you guys sleep in the same bed? And sleep together?" Most people in this modern world don't have a problem with sharing a bed or sleeping together before marriage. But Andre and I had committed to saving both of those things until our wedding day. Let me explain why we made that commitment.

From the beginning of our relationship, Andre and I both confessed that we had fallen short in the past when it came to our sexual purity. We wanted to ensure that we honored God by following what the Bible teaches about relationships between men and women, particularly when it comes to marriage. Which is what, exactly?

The Bible first mentions marriage in its second chapter, Genesis 2. There, God created Eve, the first woman, by putting Adam, the first man, to sleep and removing one of his ribs. From that rib, he formed Eve. When Adam awoke from his slumber and saw Eve, he emphatically said, "This at last is bone of my bones and flesh of my flesh; she shall be called Woman, because she was taken out of Man" (v. 23). The next verse provides the

Bible's first description of marriage. "Therefore a man shall leave his father and his mother and hold fast to his wife, and they shall become one flesh" (v. 24). What does "one flesh" mean? It means that two people are united in the most intimate and inseparable way possible—in body and soul, for life. That's what marriage is. That's one of the reasons sex before marriage is wrong, according to the Bible. (For more, check out 1 Thessalonians 4:3–5, 1 Thessalonians 5:22, and Hebrews 13:4.) It violates that lifelong commitment of the entire soul and body that God says is only for two married people. It's an amazing vision for marriage. It's a radical commitment to another that isn't common in the world today. It's a vow to love, sacrifice, and give yourself exclusively to your spouse. Andre and I wanted to honor what the Bible says about marriage, which is why we slept in separate bedrooms when he moved to Los Angeles. But after a few weeks, even that decision started to weigh on me.

The topic came up almost every day. Andre was concerned about our finances. For him, it didn't make sense to waste money on separate living arrangements when we were going to live together in a few months. I was worried about what other people would think, especially our family and close friends. Though we knew we were not crossing any lines, the thought of appearing sinful ate at my conscience.

One night after training, Andre and I were sitting at the kitchen table and our living arrangement came up again.

"Is this right?" I asked Andre, not for the first time. "Should we be sharing an apartment before we are married? I truly feel convicted about this, and it has not eased up at all."

"Why should we let other people's perceptions dictate our decisions?" he asked.

FAR BEYOND GOLD

I could tell he was frustrated. And I understand why he challenged me on that. I'd always struggled with other people's perceptions of me, especially before becoming a Christian. He knew I had a tendency to make decisions to win the approval of others, not because those decisions honored God or were the best decision for me. This could have been one of those circumstances. But I didn't think it was. I couldn't shake the idea that we weren't honoring God.

After a couple more weeks, my conscience was still bothering me, so Andre and I called the pastor who was going to marry us and asked him for counsel.

"It's not about what's convenient," he told us over a Zoom call. "The question you need to ask yourself is this: Are you submitting to God, and are you willing to sacrifice comfort and money if that's what it takes to honor him?"

Our pastor friend also reminded us that, as Christians, our reputations do matter. Not because we need others to think well of us, but because we want others to think well of Jesus. Matthew 5:16 says, "Let your light shine before others, so that they may see your good works and give glory to your Father who is in heaven."

> As Christians, our reputations do matter. Not because we need others to think well of us, but because we want others to think well of Jesus.

Though we knew what was (and was not) taking place at home, our living arrangement was not beneficial to anyone. Not to us, placing ourselves in an environment where temptation could creep in. Not for other young believers who would see that and think, *Well, if they are doing it, I guess*

174

we can too. That was not looking out for others and helping prevent them from stumbling into sin.

Now that I was a Christian, I didn't want others to think I was great. I wanted them to think my God was great and that he'd changed me. That's why reputation still mattered. I was representing Jesus, not myself. And my conscience was convinced that we would honor Christ best if Andre and I lived separately until our wedding day.

Not long after that conversation with our pastor friend, Andre moved out and didn't spend the night at the apartment again until we were married. He stayed in an extended stay hotel nearby, where he would go every evening. It was a hard decision, but one that I'm glad we made. It was an opportunity for both Andre and me to demonstrate to others, and ourselves, that we had bigger priorities than our relationship. That as much as we loved each other, we loved God more. And because we loved God more and were willing to sacrifice comfort for him, we were ready to be married and sacrifice comfort for each other.

THE BIG DAY

Finally, after what at times felt like the longest nine months of my life, it was time for the wedding. The week before the big day, I was in Philadelphia, competing at the Penn Relays, a historic track-and-field event on the campus of the University of Pennsylvania. Bobby signed me up for the 100-meter hurdles. I always enjoyed that race. It didn't last long. It wasn't the same level of pain. And it wasn't my main event, so I didn't feel as much pressure.

The day of the Penn Relay, I kept telling myself, *Get through this race, and you can get married.* I ran well and won. After the race, I felt a huge sense of relief. *Time for the biggest day of my life.* Almost as soon as I had that thought, it seemed like everything about the wedding began to spin out of my control, starting with the forecast.

As we left Philadelphia, heading back to LA for a few days before going to Virginia for the big day, I checked the weather app on my phone. My heart dropped. It was supposed to rain—downpour—the day of our wedding.

"It might change," Andre tried to reassure me. "People get the weather wrong all the time."

That's true, but this forecast said there was a 90 percent chance of thunderstorms on our wedding day. Torrential downpours, wind gusts, flooding—you name it, it was scheduled for May 6.

I was devastated. I'd always wanted an outdoor wedding, to celebrate the happiest day of my life in the sunshine. Now that wasn't a possibility. We were scrambling to try to fix the problem. We moved the ceremony and reception inside. It wasn't ideal. Not what I'd always imagined my wedding would look like. But in my moment of self-pity, a reality check set in. Marriage was more than just the day. I was marrying a person for life, rain or shine. That was what mattered, and I had to get over myself to appreciate that.

After the rehearsal dinner the night before our wedding, Andre drove me back to my hotel. I told him I was nervous. Anxious. It wasn't a case of cold feet but more like pregame jitters. Not to mention, my little brother's flight had been delayed, and he was now going to arrive the day of the wedding. So many moving parts, and so little I could do about them.

I shared my raw emotions with Andre. He listened, then offered to pray with me. I told God about my anxieties. We listened to one of our favorite songs, one that talks about telling everyone about a God of love and grace, which was exactly why we were getting married. We wanted our relationship—our marriage—to tell the whole world about Christ. We knew our marriage could do that. In fact, we believed that was the point of marriage. When Ephesians 5:31 says, "Therefore a man shall leave his father and mother and hold fast to his wife, and the two shall become one flesh," the passage continues with this statement: "This mystery is profound, and I am saying that it refers to Christ and the church" (v. 32).

As Christ loves the people of God, and in return, the people of God love Christ, so husbands love wives and wives love husbands. Incredibly, our marriage the next day was going to be a picture, for anyone watching, of Christ's love for his people. There were a thousand reasons we wanted to get married. At the top was the opportunity to love each other so people would have a picture, however small, of how God loves his people.

After we prayed and listened to a couple of worship songs, I felt at peace. I was confident we were about to honor God the next day by becoming husband and wife. And I was actually grateful for the pressures and stresses of the last few weeks. They were there because God intended them to be. And I know they were best for me, the perfect preparation for marriage.

Being married is a beautiful reality, but it's also not easy. At times, you have to let go of your vision and relinquish it, having faith in God and your spouse, and trust that different is actually better. You have to let go of the need to be in control. I certainly had to do that the week of my wedding.

> I was confident we were about to honor God the next day by becoming husband and wife.

I woke up on my wedding day with the same nervous energy I felt before a big race. Andre was the same way. We made sure to avoid seeing each other until the ceremony. I was beyond grateful for our friends and family who made us feel so loved that day. My bridesmaids were such gems in every possible way—especially my friend Danni, who helped with a lot of the plans. When I walked down the aisle, Andre couldn't hold back the tears.

The vows, the first kiss, the dinner, the dancing, the speeches from friends and family, the cake cutting, the thousands of photos all went by in a blur. Before long, it was time to leave: to end the party we'd been planning virtually nonstop for nine months.

It was the perfect day for many reasons. The dress fit perfectly. My closest friends made me feel beyond loved and celebrated. Everyone loved the indoor venue (especially because of the tornado warning outside!). In fact, they loved it so much, they said it was better than having the ceremony outside. (I'm still not ready to go quite that far.) It was incredible having everyone we loved together in one place. And it was a blast to finally be husband and wife. But what made us most happy was that God and his good news of salvation was at the center of the ceremony. Our pastor friend pointed to the cross, where Jesus laid down his life to redeem sinners. He pointed to heaven, where Christ is now, providing mercy to his people. And he explained how marriage is an opportunity for two weak, needy sinners to love each other in the same way Christ loves his church: through sacrificing for each other.

As we pulled out of the beautiful vineyard, the night sky awash in stars, our wedding was over, but our marriage had just begun. Our work as a team to honor God was a wonderful project that would last the rest of our lives together.

Chapter 11

When Andre and I returned to Los Angeles two days after our wedding, I still hadn't run a 400-meter hurdles race that season. The US National Championships were ahead of me and, if I qualified, I'd attend the World Championships one month later in the same location, my favorite place: Eugene, Oregon. This would be a heavily anticipated race for several reasons. It was the first time the World Championships were coming to American soil. There was a lot of tension riding on this meet. As the home team, we wanted to put on a show for our country. Also, this was my biggest race since the Olympics the previous summer. I had the world record, but I knew it could be broken. Several talented competitors were eager to knock me off that podium.

Everything in me wanted to win that race, and everything in me wanted to do it in such a way that I could retire from the hurdles. Don't get me wrong; I truly believe I was made for the hurdles, but the tension that your body undergoes training for that event had pushed me to my limits. I prayed that if I ran fast enough, and put the record far out of reach, I would be content moving to another event. I could find another obsession on the track, a new goal to dedicate myself to.

I was determined to make the summer of 2022 the end of one chapter and the start of another, the final page of the first half of my career and the beginning of the second half, one defined by new events and new goals. But I knew I couldn't do that if there was unfinished business at the end of the season. To move on, to feel like I'd done everything I could, I wanted to win all three races. I needed to win the World Championships. And I absolutely had to set a new world record. Just breaking it wasn't enough. I had to shatter it. Put a number up there that would stand the test of time.

I formed my goals for the 2022 season not long after Tokyo, while I was enjoying a much-needed offseason between August and early November. When Bobby and I got back on the track for the last couple of months of 2021, I was eager to resume training. If I was going to stay at the top and capture my first World Championship in 2022, I had to improve on my world record time in Tokyo, which meant training harder and running faster than I ever had before.

On day one of the new season, I told myself I hadn't accomplished anything. I reminded myself that the shiny gold medal I earned in Tokyo couldn't help me win another race. If anything, it might hurt me. Now in every race, I would be the person to beat. My success hadn't just motivated the other women; it had pushed everyone to want to beat me. Rightfully so. I now had an Olympic-gold-medal-sized target on my back.

THE GRIND

Six months into my season, and less than forty-eight hours after my wedding, I sat in a sauna in Los Angeles, hoping to somehow sweat out all the extra food I'd eaten over the weekend. The short break from training and the extra calories hadn't affected how I felt physically. I felt strong, full of energy. There was a bounce in my step, even when I wasn't training. It was the best I'd felt since the Olympics nine months ago. The path to this feeling hadn't been easy. There had even been moments when I wasn't sure if I was going to be able to pull off a successful 2022 season.

The first few months of the season, way back in December, I went back to the basics and trained as if I had to relearn every move, every strategy, every habit, and every technique that went into the 400-meter hurdles. Bobby always says, "Hurdlers hurdle." Meaning, the best way to learn is to do. In one sense, this relearning was a normal part of the process, especially with Bobby Kersee as my coach. To him, the start of the season was for building a base of strength and conditioning. It was for teaching your body how to push through the pain and ignore that voice inside that begs you to stop.

As Bobby worked to build my base, he seemed to have a knack for knowing how hard I could be pushed, when I had more in me than I realized, and especially when I had less in me than I thought. Because I was pushed to my limits each day of training, racing at the highest level felt like just another day on the track. Surviving a practice with Bobby meant I could survive anything.

Around the beginning of April 2022, five months into the season and just one month before my wedding, Bobby and I worked on some more sprint-based techniques. I felt like an athlete again. But just as that part of the season was ramping up, I noticed a disturbing feeling in my hamstring. The muscle was tight, but not just cramping tight; it felt stuck. Trying to be precautionary, we backed off for a couple of days. Days turned into weeks, and there was still a problem. I was struggling to keep my anxiety under control. All I could think about was what happened to my older brother, Taylor.

After an incredible track career at the University of Michigan, where he was an all-American in the 400-meter hurdles, Taylor was primed to make the US Olympic team in 2021. But the week before the trials, he reaggravated a hamstring during training. It wasn't something Taylor could have prevented. Hamstring injuries can strike anyone, and they can strike at the most unexpected times. Most injuries are like that. They begin as smaller issues that can snowball into something bigger. His particular injury, though, required time. Lots of time. He had to be patient. That can seem impossible when your childhood dream, and your career, depend on you getting back out on the track. Seeing my brother work so diligently to get his body healthy reminded me that this sport is a waiting game, a test of patience. Waiting for results, waiting for healing, waiting for a chance to get back out there. By the grace of God, though, almost two years after the Olympic trials, he was fully healed and ready to make another run at the games.

Having watched what my brother had gone through, I took my hamstring predicament very seriously. I had imaging and testing done. Scans showed only a minor strain. *Praise God*, I thought. But still, something was hindering me from giving 100 percent on the track. We ended up reaching out to multiple specialists to take a look at my leg. They all came to the same conclusion, diagnosing me with sciatic nerve entrapment. Somehow, a nerve had slipped out of place and became trapped in my hamstring. It was causing the tightness. We tried everything to move it: massages, wrapping tight bands around my hamstring, dry needling, shockwave therapy. Nothing seemed to work. There was only one more option left: I had to rest it. So the month of April, just as the season was ramping up, I was ramping down. Taking more days off than I would have liked. Not pushing myself on the days I did train. And fighting, day after day, to have the right attitude, to trust the process, and trust the Lord now that a lot of ambiguity surrounded my season.

God used that uncertainty to teach me yet another lesson about trusting him. Clearly, I need as many lessons as he will send my way. Sometimes when there are a lot of unknowns, and there's nothing you can do to fix the problem, you don't need to do anything extraordinary. You just need to be

> Sometimes when there are a lot of unknowns, and there's nothing you can do to fix the problem, you don't need to do anything extraordinary. You just need to be patient and wait on the Lord.

patient and wait on the Lord (Proverbs 3:5–8). Until then, faith looks like taking it a day at a time. In this case, faith looked like not getting frustrated when we couldn't find a quick solution or when I had to slow it down on the track. Faith looked like waiting. And waiting. And waiting. About a month after the tightness first appeared, it went away. What could have derailed my season had been only a speed bump. I was going to have a 2022 season.

BACK ON THE TRACK

My first race in Nashville—and my first 400-meter hurdles since Tokyo—went better than I could have hoped. Bobby wanted me to run between 53 and 52 seconds. He wasn't very concerned with all the minute details. He just wanted me to give my body and mind a much-needed refresher on racing.

Not only did I end up winning the race, but I ran it in 51.61, more than a second faster than Bobby's goal for me. I was only two-tenths of a second off the world record I'd set in Tokyo. I remember Bobby's laugh after the race. Evidently, they had placed one of the hurdles in the wrong location, so even if I had broken the world record, it would not have counted. He was also glad I didn't break it because he wasn't wearing his lucky Yankees hat. Bobby loves the Yankees. Whenever one of his runners breaks a record, he retires a hat. So on this occasion, I was glad the time did not come. I wanted him to retire the right one!

A couple of weeks after Nashville, I returned to Eugene for the US National Championships. I knew I could win if I ran the same way I did in Nashville. But thanks to the sciatic nerve in my hamstring, I wasn't sure if my body was ready for the grind of a major event with two qualifying heats and a final. Typically, there's a rest day between the semifinal and final. Not with our trials, though. The 400-meter hurdles would be run over three days. Winning wasn't just going to demand superior speed and technique. It was also going to go to the runner with an extra level of endurance. But I hadn't had much opportunity to cultivate endurance during the previous two months.

After my first heat, I realized that stamina wasn't going to be an issue. I won without having to push myself too hard. I credit Bobby for that.

After another strong performance on day two, I'd qualified for the final with the fastest time. I'd be running in lane five. Normally, my main competition, Dalilah, would be one lane behind or ahead of me. This time, she wasn't there. Since she won the last World Championships in Doha in 2019, she didn't have to qualify for the US team.

It was bright and sunny the day of the finals. Andre and I were starting to develop a routine on race day: we prayed in the morning, read together, ate breakfast, and tried to avoid talking about the upcoming race. He came with me to warm-ups but didn't say much. He seemed to sense that once it was go time, I'd be on my own. That's the stress and beauty of the sport. The people you love the most, and who love you the most, can't run the race for you. That's on you and you alone.

After a false start, the gun sounded and the finals began. I felt strong. Stronger than I thought I'd feel at the beginning of the week. I had already decided, *Today, I'm going to break the world record again.* Halfway through the race, I took the lead. It was by far the earliest I'd ever nosed ahead of the competition during a major race. I started to systematically check off hurdles, making sure I stayed in rhythm. By the time we reached the last 100 meters, I couldn't see anyone else. I didn't know how big the gap was between first and second. This was unfamiliar territory. I was typically chasing, using runners ahead of me for motivation. I didn't have that option this time. I gave it everything I had down the stretch and crossed the finish line in 51.41. That was 0.05 seconds faster than my Olympic time. *A new world record.*

Part of me was thrilled. How could I not be? I'd just set another record. But thinking through that race, I felt as though I had done everything right. So why was the time barely faster than the summer before? How could I shave off more time at the World Championships in July? Those were the questions running through my brain during the victory lap.

The World Championships may have been in the same location as US Nationals, but the intensity was on another level, especially surrounding my event. With Dalilah and me there, I'd never seen so much hype around a 400-meter hurdles race. I tried to avoid the TV coverage and stay off social media. The press was prioritizing our matchup. They had us both on world record watch.

Tokyo had certainly been pressure packed. It was the Olympics, after all. But the 2022 World Championships were the most pressure I've ever felt in my career. I was the favorite. I had the most to gain or lose. How I would prepare and handle that pressure internally would make all the difference.

RUN FOR YOUR LIFE

My family traveled from New Jersey to Eugene and packed a nearby Airbnb. Along with my parents, all three of my siblings were there with my aunt and cousins. It was a party. Since they were guaranteed to have the TV coverage running all day, and the conversation would never stray too far from the track, Andre and I rented our own house. His mom and sister flew out and joined us. It was their first time at a major track-and-field championship. We didn't talk much about track, which was exactly how I liked it the week of a big race.

For the first heat, lane assignments were chosen randomly. I drew lane eight. Not ideal. I wouldn't see my competitors. I would have no sense of where I was in the race. But that didn't matter much; my goals were advancing, getting a feel for the track as well as the crowds, and shaking off the nerves. Despite all the big races I'd competed in, I still had to deal with nerves before the first heat. The quarterfinals weren't my strongest performance, but I did advance, locking up a spot in the semifinal heat on day two.

After the first three semifinals, I knew that Femke Bol and Dalilah Muhammad were already in the final and had qualified with the two fastest times. To beat Femke, I had to run faster than 52.8 seconds, which I knew how to do. When I crossed the finish line in first place, I immediately looked at the clock to my left. It registered 52.17. That was not only the fastest qualifying time, which meant I would get the best lane for the final, but it was also 0.01 seconds off Dalilah's World Championship record in Doha three years ago. I felt good.

I didn't want to wait two days for the final. I would have run it that night if I could. I felt better than I'd ever felt physically. And I just wanted the race to be over with.

Dealing with the tension over the next two days was mentally exhausting. The race would be won in the waiting. How I coped, how I prepared, how I recovered—that's where the championship would lie. Those two days were, without a doubt, the toughest part of the week. The final was going to be the most important race of my life; I was certain of that. If I won and broke the world record, I could leave the 400-meter hurdles behind. If I didn't, I wouldn't be able to leave the event until I got another shot at a World Championship.

The day before the finals, there were moments when I felt tears starting to well up. It was too much pressure. Anytime Andre saw that, he stepped in and encouraged me, reminded me of what was true, reminded me that God was in control. His encouragement included reminders of the verse in Hebrews we had been reciting that whole week: "So let us come *boldly* to the throne of our gracious God. There we will receive his mercy, and we will find grace to help us when we need it most" (4:16 NLT). Andre reminded me to be bold. To approach God with confidence in the assurance of my faith and receive his grace to help me in my time of need.

Bobby called and talked as if the race were already over and I'd accomplished my goals. All I had to do was go out on the track and do what we'd talked about over and over. His wife, the great Jackie Joyner-Kersee, called and echoed her husband's encouragement. By the time I headed to bed that night, my eyes were dry. I was locked in and ready to compete. I'd come so far since I had first run in a final on this track six years ago. I was a woman now. I didn't race for myself. I didn't find my identity on the track. I had a remarkable family, coach, and friends who supported me and pointed me away from my feelings of inadequacy and toward truth that was outside myself—that God had me, no matter what, and he had a plan. *I've never been more ready*, I told myself.

As I stood at the starting blocks the following evening, pacing back and forth with more energy than I knew what to do with, the camera zoomed in. I didn't notice it. My mind was already on the track. The instinct had already kicked in.

> God had me, no matter what, and he had a plan.

Dalilah was in lane six, one ahead of me. Femke was one behind me, in lane four. My two main competitors were right where I needed them to be: Dalilah ahead of me, and Femke chasing.

The gun sounded, and I shot out of the starting blocks. I reached hurdle one first. Then I reached the second one before anyone else. By the time we reached the midpoint of the race, I'd nosed ahead of Dalilah. This was the point when I tended to coast as I prepared for the final push. *Not today,* I told myself. *Attack everything.*

Strategy went out the window as I opened a lead. I could have been risking exhaustion down the final 100 meters, but I didn't care. I wasn't holding anything back. This was it. I felt as if this was the last race I'd ever run.

We reached the final stretch, and I felt strong. I cleared hurdle eight, no problem. I was ready for the final kick. The crowd, ten thousand strong, roared and rose to its feet. I couldn't see my competitors, but I felt as if they were right behind me, Dalilah on my right shoulder and Femke on my left. The energy was electric. I stumbled a bit on hurdle nine as lactic acid began to take over my body. But I landed in rhythm on the other side of the hurdle. *One more to go,* I thought. *Run for your life.* My legs started to tighten. My energy, so strong moments before, started to fade. I couldn't feel anything as I went over the last hurdle. *Just don't hit it,* I told myself. When I landed, my legs nearly buckled. I had nothing left. Nothing but willpower. *Run for your life*, I said again.

Andre showed me a replay of the race later that night. I was shocked. The tape showed no one was close, but in the moment, I could have sworn I heard footsteps. I'd panicked, knowing I had nothing left to give and thinking either Dalilah or Femke was stalking me, about to zip past me, and there was nothing I could do about it. But that hadn't happened. As I watched the replay, I felt like I was watching God put a fence around me as I stumbled and leaned entirely on him as I crossed the finish line.

As soon as I finished and saw that I'd set another world record with a time of 50.68, my legs buckled. I crouched down. "Thank you, God," I said over and over. It's all I had the strength to say. It was all I needed to say. At that moment, I didn't care about the World Championship. I didn't care about my time. I only cared that I'd run the race the way I was supposed to. I'd given it everything I had. I'd left the results in God's hands.

That's what was so defining about that moment. Yes, it was wonderful to set a new record. Yes, the World Championship was amazing. But I felt waves of joy because Hebrews 4:16 came to fruition. God gave me grace and mercy. After weeks of me laying this burden at his feet, the Lord helped me through one of the toughest trials I had ever faced. God had delivered me from the anxiety of failing. He'd replaced it with faith in him, faith in the process, faith that if I trusted him and ran the way he'd made me to, I wouldn't be ashamed, even if I had lost.

At the World Championships in 2022, I'd run with confidence. Not confidence in myself. I'd tried that in the past, and it had led only to crippling anxiety and lackluster performances. Instead, I'd run with confidence in God and his promises. I'd learned that in racing, and in life, God gives you exactly what you need to run the race he has for you. He gives grace and help to all those who look to him, not themselves, for strength, courage, peace, and joy. He helped me grow spiritually that day by testing where my faith truly was. I grew closer to the Lord through that lap in Eugene. That was the icing on it all. I'd needed his grace those last 50 meters on the track. He kept me on my feet and pushed me across the finish line. All the glory goes to him.

> God had delivered me from the anxiety of failing. He'd replaced it with faith in him.

Chapter 12

After Eugene, Andre and I finally got to take our honeymoon. We got to be husband and wife without a major competition looming. For a few months, the days were slower and the time together was sweet as fall became winter and 2022 drew to a close.

Each Sunday, we enjoyed fellowship with our new friends at church. The people and the teaching refreshed our souls. Our pastor preached what are called expository sermons. The idea is simple: the pastor opens the Bible and explains it, verse by verse, line by line, phrase by phrase. The primary focus is not on cultural events. You don't worry about politics, pop culture, or news headlines. Week after week, you study the same book of the Bible, slowly looking at what it meant to the people who first read it thousands of years ago. Andre and I both felt like we were learning more about the Bible, and Jesus, than we ever had before.

At our new church, there's a graduate school—a seminary—that trains pastors. When we learned about the program, it felt like a divine appointment. Andre had been thinking about attending seminary, and God placed an amazing one right in our local church. I loved the idea of him as a pastor. I don't know anyone more passionate about studying the Bible and teaching it to others than Andre. Love God and love people—that's Andre in a nutshell. And that's exactly what a pastor does with his life. Andre applied and was accepted with a full scholarship. And the first week of 2023, he began classes at The Master's Seminary.

As Andre settled into his new school and I took a break from training, I started to think about my goals, how I could best serve and glorify God, both on and off the track. I wondered, *Does God still want me to use my gifts on the track? Do I still have that competitive edge?*

BIG GOALS

As I thought about those questions, I realized that I still loved to compete. In fact, even today, in some ways I'm more competitive than I've ever been in my life. After 2022, a new sense of purpose has emerged within me. The opportunities afforded to me through track and field present a platform to proclaim Christ. That is the goal: hold the microphone as long as I can and use it to share the good news of the gospel.

Before committing my life to Jesus, I had no idea how motivating it is to run for someone else: to have a purpose for my career that goes far beyond my success. Knowing that running is a gift from God motivates me to use the gift well, not to waste what I've been given. It makes track more fulfilling, knowing that it doesn't all depend on me. The Bible assumes that runners like me run for a reason. "Do you not know that in a race all the runners run, but only one receives the prize? So run that you may obtain it. Every athlete exercises self-control in all things. They do it to receive a perishable wreath, but we an imperishable. So I do not run aimlessly; I do not box as one beating the air. But I discipline my body and keep it under control, lest after preaching to others I myself should be disqualified" (1 Corinthians 9:24–27).

When we run the race of faith, we do it to obtain the prize of God's glory and eternity with him in heaven. Here on earth, I run to win, to obtain the prize in track and field for the glory of God. And to do that, I still need goals. So what are my goals, my dreams, for the second half of my career on the track?

As I write this chapter in the summer of 2023, I am eager to see what the Lord has for me, but I also know that God's presence does not mean the absence of problems. My 2023 season came to a close in the most uneventful way. Due to a recurring issue with my left knee, I had to withdraw from the World Championships in Budapest, Hungary. Months and months of training for this one moment, gone in the blink of an eye. It is a tough pill to swallow knowing

> When we run the race of faith, we do it to obtain the prize of God's glory and eternity with him in heaven.

that I didn't lose the race, but I didn't even get the chance to step on the line. Still, I rejoice (James 5:13). I mourn for the dream I had envisioned for this year. For the anticipation of building on the previous year's momentum. I weep for the lost opportunity for my team, friends, and family to experience this championship with me as we chase God's glory.

Yet I am at peace. Not just peace but joy. I rejoice in this year's lessons. The personal character that was developed through perseverance. The bonds that were strengthened between me and those closest to me. Ultimately, the Lord humbled me. God often prunes us in very unexpected ways (John 15:2). Though believers may feel we haven't done anything "wrong" to deserve the trials we face, it is for our good that we face the storm. If anything, failure is now an opportunity, a chance to show others that winning is not my ultimate priority. Even in the lowest moments on the track, I can know that God has a purpose for me, and I can find fulfilment in his plan. First Corinthians 10:31 says it beautifully: "So, whether you eat or drink, or whatever you do, do all to the glory of God." That "whatever you do" includes winning or losing.

At this point in my life, I have no idea how long I will run, how successful I'll be, or what events I'll compete in. And I'm okay with the uncertainty. I've learned to embrace the fact that I'm not in control of the future. God may have track victories in my future, or he may not. All I can do is be faithful with today. I can work hard. And perhaps more importantly, I can enjoy the process.

No one becomes a track-and-field athlete for the money. There's not a crazy amount of it in our sport, like there is in basketball or football. No one does it for the fame. Not a ton of that either. And while running can feel good—especially when your body releases endorphins—it almost always produces an extraordinary amount of pain. You can barely breathe. You are stiff and sore later that night. So while the money, fame, and pleasure of running may not be all that attractive, there's another element that pulls athletes like me into the sport. I must confess that I'm hopelessly addicted to the process of improvement. In running, there's no better feeling than knowing that today, I'm better than I was yesterday—and if I put in the work now, I'll be even better tomorrow. Hardly anything is more satisfying than setting a goal—especially one that seems impossible—and patiently pursuing it until you cross that goal off your to-do list.

Because of my newfound love for Jesus, I see so much more purpose and pleasure in the process of reaching those goals. The long days of training cultivate patience and self-control, the fruit of the Spirit (Galatians 5:22–23). Every workout and race is given to him in prayer. I pray for strength and courage in my mind, body, and spirit. I pray that God's will would be done and that I would have the perseverance to obey him. I truly believe that my days on the track bring God pleasure. I didn't always feel that way. Before I was a Christian, and even after it for a while, I would think, *I'm not really working a real job. I'm not being productive, helping society, building something or doing anything that makes life better for people. I'm just an athlete.*

> Because of my newfound love for Jesus, I see so much more purpose and pleasure in the process of reaching those goals.

I don't think that anymore. Now I see that running is God's plan for my life. He gave me this gift. He gave me a platform. I tell people all the time, there is a responsibility that comes with that. No matter who you are or what you do, what is in your heart pours out. How you present yourself is a representation of who you serve, whether God or other people. For me, I intentionally try my best to make sure people don't see Sydney Michelle McLaughlin-Levrone, but they see Christ working through a young track runner to bring himself glory. Using my mind, body, and soul to compete at the highest level is biblical. He made me to do this, and whether that means more gold medals and world records or failing to qualify for future World Championships and Olympics, I know the act of running and competition honors him. He has a plan for each person he created. He gave me, you, and everyone a drive to do something—something that can be used for his glory and bring both you and him joy in the process. Whatever we do, making sure it honors God is the highest and most fulfilling way to live. Whatever may come day by day, we can do it for him.

> Whatever we do, making sure it honors God is the highest and most fulfilling way to live.

FUTURE GENERATIONS

When I think about my life after the track, I dream of starting a family, of being a mom. When this will happen, I don't know. But Shelly-Ann Fraser-Pryce, Nia Ali, and a host of other women have shown that not only can you compete again after becoming a mom, but you can come back to the sport stronger.

If and when that happens I will leave to the Lord's timing, but the desire is strong in my heart. I'm learning to trust God with the future, knowing that he cares for me and Andre, and he knows what is best for us.

When Andre finishes seminary and my time training with Bobby comes to a close, we want to move east, to the coast we are from. Andre wants to be a pastor and care for all people, regardless of their skin color, age, or wealth. He wants to preach the Bible week after week, tell people about Jesus, and then help them honor God each and every day. And when my career is over, I want to mentor children. Share some of the lessons and wisdom I have accumulated over the years. Help them avoid some of the same mistakes I made.

I've already had the incredible opportunity to do that. Girls who are a few years younger than I am have reached out and asked me for advice. I love helping in some small way. Recently, I got to know a high school girl who competes on a track team in Southern California. We happened to meet at UCLA. Both of us were there, working with my trainer. I'll never forget Andre telling her to stay away from knuckleheads, guys who have not matured yet in their thinking. Instead, he told her to focus on the path God has her on, to seek the Lord, and keep running the race of life faithfully. Months later, she reached out to me because she was struggling with hurdles during her high school season.

"I don't have all the answers," I told her, remembering when my hurdling technique was a mess. "But I know someone who can help."

Bobby graciously agreed to meet with her a few times. He has a heart for youth as much as I do, and it was nice seeing the wisdom he's instilled in me passed on to others. All her life updates made me smile and reminded me of the girl I once was. Even though I am only five or six years older than her, she reminded me so much of my younger self. It was a thrill to be able to help her in some way and know that helping others doesn't always mean having the answers. But true care is giving what you can, while you can.

MY BIGGEST LESSONS

Through these kinds of conversations and others like them, I've thought a lot about the best advice I can give. The advice I wish I'd had and heeded when I was younger. And what's that?

The number one piece of advice is simple: *life is better with Jesus.* I truly believe that. For so long I'd tried to run my life without him. I'd tried to control my destiny, find happiness on my own. It didn't work. I was anxious, depressed, frustrated, and lonely before Christ. I know not everyone shares my beliefs. I get that. But no matter who you are or what background you come from, that's my encouragement to you. Life is better with Jesus. He promises peace and rest to all who trust him. He promises forgiveness to all who repent, believe that he died on the cross for their sins, and trust in him for eternal life. Knowing that, I'm much better able to handle the trials and anxieties that inevitably are part of life (Romans 6:23, John 17:3, Philippians 4:6–7). If I have a bad day, whether on the track or not, I can know that it's temporary, that one day my trials will be no more because of what Jesus did for me on the cross.

My second piece of advice, especially for those stepping into adulthood, is this: *don't run from trials and difficult circumstances.* I spent most of my early life doing that. I ran from the Olympics in 2016. I ran from the high school drama and the challenges I faced in college. I even tried to escape from the crushing losses in 2019 back into a relationship that was terrible for me. So much can be learned from pruning seasons. They teach us endurance. They cultivate patience. Ultimately, they require dependence on the one who can lead us through—Christ.

Life is better with Jesus.

Looking back, I'm so thankful I qualified for the 2016 Olympics, and even for the mess that came after. If I hadn't had that experience in Rio, I don't think I would have known what to expect, how to prepare, and how to compete in Tokyo. Would I have won gold in Tokyo if I hadn't competed in Rio? Maybe. But I know for certain my experience in Rio helped me prepare to achieve my dreams five years later.

I'm also grateful for my year at the University of Kentucky. It was tough. It was upsetting. Easily one of the hardest years of my life. If I had gone to USC, I might have been happier, yet I may have dealt with different adversities there than I did at UK. God let me explore the options I had been considering, but ultimately, he led me right to where I needed to be.

I'm also grateful for those crushing defeats in 2019 at the US Nationals and World Championships. If I had won, I don't know if I would have seen a need to make a change professionally—or mentally, physically, and spiritually. I don't know if I would have turned to Bobby. More importantly, I don't know if or when I would have turned to God. I'm grateful that God knew what was best for me was not what I desperately wanted the summer of 2019.

Finally, I'm grateful for my journey in the first half of 2020. Not long after the Olympics was canceled, I hit rock bottom. I had nowhere to turn. I was lonely, anxious, and desperate for help. After I didn't find what I was looking for in therapy, I finally turned to God. He used the isolation of COVID and the recent heartaches in Doha and failed relationships to bring me to himself, so I could begin to understand how to make him the priority. If that process hadn't begun in the early part of that year, I don't know if I would have been ready for a relationship with Andre when we met that August.

Through those trials, God has taught me so much. Though they were all difficult, exhausting, emotional experiences, I'm grateful for them. They helped me understand how to rely on Christ, not myself, in any situation. They were refining me into the woman God has called me to be.

My third and final piece of wisdom would be simply this: *you don't need to be afraid if you have Jesus.* For so many years, fear ruled me. I didn't have true hope. I thought there was no escaping the anxiety and fear. I assumed that's how life was always going to be because I thought it was my job, my responsibility, to get rid of my fear. I had no clue how to do that. Then Christ saved me.

> You don't need to be afraid if you have Jesus.

He taught me that my identity is in him, not in my achievements, relationships, words, or physical features. He taught me how to love others, pursue running with all my strength, and respond with grace and kindness, win or lose. Fear is a product of misplaced priorities. It comes from valuing the wrong thing too much. But when you value Jesus above all else, he takes your fear and replaces it with faith (Philippians 4:6–7).

The whole purpose and central motivation of my life, as the Westminster Catechism says, "is to glorify God, and to enjoy him forever."[12] It's not about what medals I win or how history will remember my career. It's far beyond gold. It's about glorifying God the Father and his Son, Jesus Christ, through whom the Spirit works to bring redemption to those lost in sin.

> Fear is a product of misplaced priorities. It comes from valuing the wrong thing too much. But when you value Jesus above all else, he takes your fear and replaces it with faith.

No matter what I encounter in years to come, no matter what trials and fears I may face, I know that following him is my way forward. Until then, I'm committed to running the good race, for his glory.

Acknowledgments

I would be remiss if I didn't take a moment to acknowledge that it was God's grace that made sharing my story possible. Along with that comes an army of supportive, loving, and encouraging people who have believed in me every step of the way.

My greatest thanks to Corey Williams and Suzanne Gosselin for their help in crafting my story onto the pages that you see now. As well as my deep appreciation to HarperCollins for allowing me the opportunity to share my testimony with the world.

Thank you to my loving husband, Andre, for all your reassurance and aid during this process. You are a pillar of faithfulness in my life. Finally, my great appreciation for my family: I love you all dearly.

God bless.

Notes

1. NBC Sports, "16-Year-Old Sydney McLaughlin's Spectacular Debut at 2016 Olympic Trials | NBC Sports," October 2, 2020, YouTube, 0:44 to 0:51, https://www.youtube.com/watch?v=cIDvMLwX2N4.
2. Chad Konecky, "Sydney McLaughlin Dishes about Chocolate Bars, the Olympic Trials, and Turning Pro," *USA Today*, June 27, 2016, https://usatodayhss.com/2016/sydney-mclaughlin-dishes-about-chocolate-bars-the-olympic-trials-and-turning-pro.
3. "Sydney McLaughlin: Prodigy," FloTrack, May 16, 2017, video, 15:30, https://www.flotrack.org/collections/6751352-sydney-mclaughlin-prodigy?playing=5829907.
4. NBC Sports, "Dalilah Muhammad Breaks World Record in 400 Hurdles at US Nationals | NBC Sports," July 28, 2019, YouTube, 0:13 to 0:16, https://www.youtube.com/watch?v=ZdfDJN4sPbI.
5. Andre Levrone Jr. (@andrelevrone), "My hope is not in the path," Instagram post, October 4, 2018, https://www.instagram.com/p/Boh3f-UhJ9G/.

6. Andre Levrone Jr. (@andrelevrone), "66 books written by over 40 authors," Instagram post, June 18, 2019, https://www.instagram.com/p/By3vSiVgiF2/.

7. Andrew Levrone Jr. (@andrelevrone), "My parents been holding each other down since 1984," Instagram post, October 27, 2014, https://www.instagram.com/p/urT9sxteyR/.

8. See also Luke 8:48; 17:19; 18:42.

9. Hugh Hudson, dir., *Chariots of Fire*, (UK), 20th Century Fox, 1981.

10. Corrie ten Boom, *Each New Day: 365 Reflections to Strengthen Your Faith* (1977; repr., Grand Rapids: Revell, 2013), 78.

11. Sydney McLaughlin (@sydneymclaughlin16), "Dear future husband," Instagram post, August 25, 2021, https://www.instagram.com/p/CTAabQ2J4pL/.

12. Adapted from William Carruthers, *The Shorter Catechism of the Westminster Assembly of Divines* (London: The Presbyterian Church of England, 1897), 1, https://archive.org/details/shortercatechis00west/page/n11/.

About the Author

Sydney McLaughlin-Levrone is a four-time Olympian and world record-holding American sprinter and hurdler. At just 16, she made the U.S. Olympic team for the 2016 Rio Summer Olympics, becoming the youngest U.S. track and field Olympian since 1972. During the Olympic trials, she set a junior world record in the 400m hurdles.

McLaughlin-Levrone solidified her place as a track superstar at the 2021 Tokyo Olympics, winning gold in the 400m hurdles with a world record time of 51.46 seconds, as well as another gold in the 4x400m relay.

At the 2024 Paris Olympics, she further cemented her status as a track and field legend by becoming the first woman to win consecutive gold medals in the 400m hurdles, breaking her own world record for the sixth time with a time of 50.37 seconds. She followed this up just days later with another gold in the 4x400m relay.

Before turning professional, McLaughlin-Levrone competed at the University of Kentucky and was named Gatorade National High School Track and Field Athlete of the Year for two consecutive years (2015-2016, 2016-2017). Born in Dunellen, New Jersey, she now resides in Los Angeles, California, with her husband, Andre Levrone, Jr.